Victorious Bible Curriculum

THE BEGINNING (PART 1 OF 9)

God created a home for mankind, and placed us in it to tend and guard it as His image. When we rebelled, God promised a seed of the woman to one day restore creation — and preserved that seed when our violence filled the world.

THE PATRIARCHS (PART 2 OF 9)

God chose Abraham to be the custodian of the line through which the promised redeemer would come. Abraham's grandson Jacob became the father of the twelve tribes of Israel, a nation that would bless the whole earth.

THE EXODUS (PART 3 OF 9)

For 400 years, God grew Jacob's tiny family into a nation. Through Moses, He released them from slavery to give them a new home. Despite the faithless first generation's rebellion, their children would inherit the promised land.

CONQUEST AND JUDGMENT (PART 4 OF 9)

Under Joshua, the children of the exodus conquered the promised land. After they settled in, they fell into idolatry and suffered under foreign domination. Time after time, they needed God's deliverance through a head-crushing judge.

THE KINGDOM OF ISRAEL (PART 5 OF 9)

God used Israel's first kings, the vacillating Saul and the head-crusher David, to give Israel peace. Solomon built a prosperous kingdom, which then split and fell into idolatry. After 70 years' exile in Babylon, God restored them to the land.

THE COMING OF THE MESSIAH (PART 6 OF 9)

The long wait for the serpent-crushing redeemer came to an end with the birth of Jesus of Nazareth. Raised in Galilee and baptized in the Jordan, He began to proclaim the kingdom of God and demonstrate God's love and power.

THE MINISTRY OF JESUS (PART 7 OF 9)

The blind could see, the sick were healed, the dead raised. The kingdom of God was truly at hand. But the leaders of Israel rejected the One God had sent to save them from their sins and deliver them into God's kingdom.

JESUS' FINAL DAYS (PART 8 OF 9)

On Thursday, before His arrest, Jesus ate one final meal with His disciples. Then He was arrested, beaten, falsely accused, tried, convicted and crucified. But death could not hold Him and the grave could not contain Him.

THE BEGINNING OF THE CHURCH (PART 9 OF 9)

After His resurrection, Jesus' followers received the power of the Holy Spirit to disciple the nations of the world, baptizing them and teaching them all that Jesus had said. Christ's body grew and began to crush the enemy's head under her feet.

Copyright © 2016 by Joe Anderson and Tim Nichols

All rights reserved
Printed in the United States of America
First Edition

No part of this book may be reproduced in any form or by any electronic or mechanical means, including information storage and retrieval systems, except for brief quotations in printed reviews, without the prior permission of the author.

Unless otherwise indicated, all Scripture quotations are taken from the New King James Version®. Copyright © 1982 by Thomas Nelson, Inc. Used by permission. All rights reserved.

Scripture quotations marked (NIV) are taken from the Holy Bible, New International Version®, NIV®. Copyright © 1973, 1978, 1984, 2011 by Biblica, Inc.™ Used by permission of Zondervan. All rights reserved worldwide. www.zondervan.com The "NIV" and "New International Version" are trademarks registered in the United States Patent and Trademark Office by Biblica, Inc.™

Author's translation or paraphrase indicated by an asterisk after the reference.

Illustrations by Gustave Doré
Colorized and modified by William Britton

Praise for Headwaters Bible Curriculum

These lessons are not just a way to teach the Bible to middle school kids. As I read the lessons, I found both my head and my heart irresistibly engaged. Joe and Tim have opened the grace and truth of God's Word in a way that seriously lifts us towards Christ while nudging us outward towards the world. I recommend these studies for both devotional and motivational reading!

Dave Cheadle, President of the Rocky Mountain Classis, Reformed Church of America

While I have spent quite a bit of time studying the Bible myself, I find your ideas and themes to be real food for thought and they help tie together much of the story God is telling throughout... I've already talked with people about your curriculum and have recommended they look into it for their own families. I can't loan out my copy for their perusal, because I'm using it everyday!

Linda Kidder, Home Educator, Colorado

I LOVE THIS BOOK!!!! We're just finishing up the Garden narrative. We've had such fruitful discussions—I have been pleased with it in every way. In fact, I'm hoping our church will start using it. I haven't had any problems or difficulties using the curriculum, I ONLY have good things to say about it. In fact, I'm in danger of writing in all caps I'm so enthusiastic about it.

Leah Robinson, Home Educator, Texas

I am really enjoying having this resource to work from and steer our lessons!

Christy Johnson, Bible Teacher, Bingham Academy, Ethiopia

Our family actually loves the curriculum. My children are in 5th and 8th grade and the content has suited both of their levels perfectly. To this point we hadn't found a curriculum that taught the Bible at such a detailed level that has also kept the kids engaged. We've had to slow down on the materials because otherwise they would be through them well before the school year is up. We are planning on buying the rest of the series.

Chris Turner, Home Educator, Colorado

How to Use This Book

This series of little manuals walks you through the biblical Story from end to end. Just read. Here are a few things you might want to keep in mind as you read through the Story.

- Try to love the characters. God does....
- The story is written in such a way as to make sin look stupid, but remember that the characters are all real people. No matter how stupid the choice, a real person actually looked at the options and then picked that particular one for reasons that seemed pretty good at the time. Nobody gets up in the morning and says, "I'm going to make stupid life choices that people will be mocking for centuries." Try to see it from their point of view. Ask yourself, "Why did this look like a good idea at the time?" That's how you learn to recognize temptations. It's easy to see sinful and stupid choices for what they are in hindsight, but in the moment it's often very hard. So learn to think through what these choices looked like from the inside, in the heat of the moment — you'll be amazed what you learn about yourself.
- Pay attention to the patterns. We'll point out a bunch of them as we go through the Story, but try to spot them yourself, too. If you can learn to read the Word and see the patterns in the Story, you will become able to read the world around you and see the patterns in the story God is telling right now.
- Each lesson comes with a psalm. The psalms provide us with another lens through which to look at the Story, and God has a lot to teach us that way. Sometimes we've given you an activity that will help integrate the psalm with that episode in the Story. Other times, we've just given you the psalm, and we're going to let you fill in the blanks. Read over the psalm a few times, then go into the lesson and see what comes to you. You'll be surprised what you can learn.
- As with any book that talks about Scripture, don't necessarily take our word for anything. Imagine you're sitting in a living room or around a campfire with us, and we're just talking about the Story. You're free to disagree, correct, challenge our understanding. The Word is the authority, not us — so grab your Bible and look things up yourself.

You'll find a section labeled "Activities" following the lesson. The point of this section is to immerse you as deeply in the Story as possible, through prayer, meditation on the Story, and other exercises. The "Evaluation" questions at the end of each lesson will help you to check your understanding of the material.

For Small Group Leaders
Have everyone in the group read the lesson ahead of time. Depending on how involved your group is, you can have them engage some or all of the activities, or you can save those for group time when you're together. The evaluation questions might serve as discussion starters if the conversation lags.

For Homeschoolers
Have your student read the lesson and complete the activities. (Some might be more appropriate as whole-family activities.) You can use the evaluation questions as a quiz or as discussion starters to check your student's comprehension of the lesson.

Table of Contents

Unit 1 Creation and Fall ... 7
    Lesson 1.1 A Home for Mankind: God Formed the Heavens and the Earth ... 9
    Lesson 1.2 A Home for Mankind: God Filled the Heavens and the Earth ... 17
    Lesson 1.3 Kings and Queens of Creation: The Purpose of Mankind ... 23
    Lesson 1.4 Training Ground: The Man as Priest and Protector of the Garden ... 29
    Lesson 1.5 The King's Companion: The Creation of Woman ... 35
    Lesson 1.6 The Serpent's Attack: The Temptation of Eve and the Failure of the King ... 41
    Lesson 1.7 Relationships Broken Between the King, His Companion and Their God ... 49
    Lesson 1.8 The Hope of Restoration: The Seed Will Crush the Serpent's Head ... 55
    Lesson 1.9 Consequences: Pain in Childbearing, Toil, Expulsion from the Garden ... 61

Unit 2 Humanity Poisoned ... 69
    Lesson 2.1 Eve's Hope Delayed—The First Seed Murdered by a Serpent: Cain and Abel ... 71
    Lesson 2.2 Cain's Wicked Line and a New Seed-Line Chosen ... 77
    Lesson 2.3 The Flood ... 83
    Lesson 2.4 God's Covenant with Noah and the New Creation ... 91
    Lesson 2.5 The Babylon Project—A Godless City Destroyed: The Tower of Babel ... 97

UNIT 1: CREATION AND FALL

In the beginning God created the heavens and the earth, forming the world as a home for mankind and then filling it with heavenly lights and animals of every kind. On the sixth day, God created mankind as His (relational and plural) image, and blessed them to multiply and rule over creation. These are not jobs one man can do by himself, and God took Adam through an exercise where he learned his need for a helper, which God then provided for him. God placed the man and woman in a garden where they could learn their responsibilities, giving them tasks to do and commands to obey. God set the seventh day aside for rest.

Having established Adam as priest and king-in-training in the garden, God then provided a test for the man and the woman, forbidding them to eat from one specific tree, the tree of the knowledge of good and evil, because they would die if they ate from it. The serpent deceived the woman, and she ate from the tree; Adam willfully sinned and also ate from the tree. The man and the woman now knew good and evil and had given the serpent their authority over creation.

Eating from the tree broke the relationship between Adam and Eve; they knew they were naked and tried to cover themselves. It also broke their relationship with God, and when He came to the garden, they hid. When God approached them, Adam blamed Eve and God, and Eve blamed the serpent. God responded by setting the process of redemption in motion. He promised that a descendant of the woman would crush the head of the serpent, returning mankind to their rightful place as rulers over creation. God then explained the consequences of their sin: Eve would have great pain in childbirth and a frustrated desire to rule over her husband, and for Adam's sake, the earth itself was cursed and would only produce fruit with great toil, until finally Adam returned to dust at the end of his days.

In spite of the inevitable suffering and death he was facing, Adam seized God's promise of a seed to crush the serpent's head and named his wife Eve, because she would be the mother of all the living. God helped launch Adam and Eve into their new life outside the garden, performing the first sacrifice and making them coverings and royal garments. He then sent them out to work the ground east of the garden. As a final protection, God set an angel with a flaming sword to guard the way to the garden, so they would not eat from the tree of life without first passing through death.

LESSON 1.1

A Home for Mankind: God Formed the Heavens and the Earth

THE STORY

Lesson Theme—God's fourfold creation process
Genesis 1 is profoundly important for Christians for a variety of reasons. In regards to apologetic concerns, Genesis 1 gives us the background for the redemption of all creation. Furthermore, it provides an alternative to the competing creation narratives, both ancient chaos and order stories as well as the modern atheistic evolutionary narrative. These are important points, but for our purposes, we want to focus on Genesis 1 as the DNA of all biblical stories. The things we see God doing in Genesis 1 in the process of creating the heavens and the earth are the very same things He did in the life of Abraham, the nation of Israel, and the life of the Messiah. The finished products of God's creative work are brought through creation to maturity through a fourfold process in which God commands, divides, names and evaluates.

In the beginning...God
In the ancient creation stories, the gods were not separate from creation but a part of it. In some cases, the universe itself was made out of the bodies of the gods (see the Accadian myth, Enuma Elish). In the modern story of evolution, *nothing* existed before creation and all that was made was made from *nothing by no one*. In contrast to both of these narratives, Genesis 1 starts out with a transcendent God creating all things out of nothing. In verse one, God was outside of creation... creating it. In verse two, His Spirit was hovering over the waters, both separate from creation and immediately present within it. In verse three, God spoke and we are introduced

OVERVIEW

In the beginning God created the heavens and the earth as a home for mankind. In the first three days of creation, God formed the universe. He created through a fourfold process of commanding, dividing, naming and evaluating. In these three days, God created and divided light and darkness, water, and land and sea. He also commanded the earth to bring forth vegetation.

SOURCE MATERIAL

- Genesis 1:1-13
- Psalms 29, 148
- Proverbs 3:19

(albeit obliquely) to the Word of God, the third member of the Trinity.

In the verses following, the Triune God created the world following the fourfold pattern mentioned above. On each day, He commanded something into existence, divided that which was newly created, named the divided parts and then evaluated His creation. Again, this structure will be important throughout the Old Testament, so make a mental note. It's amazing to see the careful process by which God formed the world; truly, He formed it in wisdom (Prov 3:19).

God spoke and it was so
Throughout the creation process, God spoke and it was so. God's words are obvious on the command part: "Then God said, 'Let there be light'"

Unit 1: Creation and Fall

OBJECTIVES

Feel...

- awe at God's power in creation.
- gratitude for the perfectly suited environment that God made for man.

Understand...

- that God made everything that is.
- that the universe obeys God when He speaks.
- God's fourfold creative activity: speaking/commanding, dividing, naming, evaluating.
- that the Trinity is evident in creation.

Apply this understanding by...

- thanking God for forming a suitable home (earth) for you to live in.
- praising God for the beauty and majesty of the creation.

the waters to divide; He commanded the land to bring forth plants, and so on, and they obeyed (cf. Ps 148:5).

In each day of creation, God divided His creation. Francis Schaeffer used to say that one of the most important things about the God of the Bible is that all things are not the same to Him. Dividing is a major theme of God's activity in history. Indeed, God divided Abraham from Ur, Israel from Egypt, the priests from Israel, the high priest from the priesthood. Furthermore, we are divided from the world and called for a specific purpose. Some of the typological links are easy to see (e.g., God dividing light from darkness equates to dividing holiness from sin), and others are harder to see (e.g., How does dividing land and sea relate to sanctification?). Many of these things will become clear later on.

After dividing, God named what He had created. Both commanding and naming are speech, but they perform different functions. Naming is

(Gen 1:3), but God's speech was equally present in some of the other aspects of God's creative process. In verse six, He divided the waters from the waters by speaking, and in verse eight, God *called* the firmament heaven. God spoke, and it was so. In our relationship with God, He speaks and it changes us. God commands us to do things, divides us from the world and names us His righteous sons and daughters so that one day He might glorify us. His words spoken to us are just as authoritative as His creative work in Genesis 1.

Command, divide, name, evaluate
Working through Genesis 1:1-13, we see God commanding the world into existence. God commanded the universe, and it was created. He commanded that there be light; He commanded

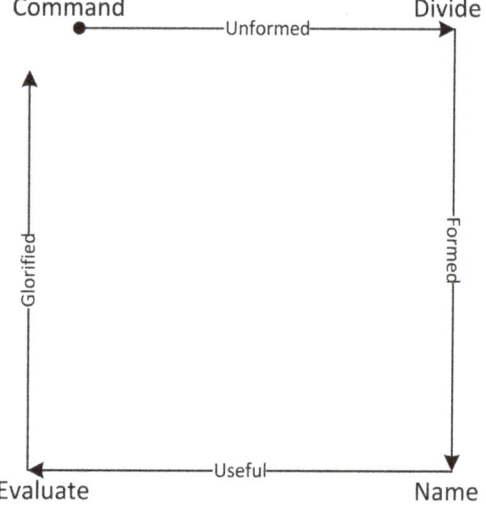

Figure 1.1 *God's fourfold creative activity*

about authority; to name something is to assert authority over it and claim responsibility for it. Naming also describes the nature of the named thing or person and establishes its purpose. God named during the creation, but it was hardly the last time. God's right to name His creation is a significant theme throughout the Bible.

Also notice where God stopped naming the creation (the middle of the third day). He named the basic constituents of the environment (day and night, sky and land and sea), but left the plants (and later the animals) to man, who would govern the creation as God's image.

Finally, after commanding, dividing and naming, God evaluated His creation. You'll notice, however, that this was not true of every day of creation; at the end of days one and two we don't see anything about God finding creation good (i.e., no evaluation). God did not begin to call His creation good until He made the dry land—the place where man was going to live. "God saw that it was good" (Gen 1:10) is an evaluation of the land's fitness for a purpose, and the purpose was to make a home for man. (Also note that in the middle of day one, God saw that the light was good, which appears to be an anomaly. Why did God evaluate in the middle of day one, but not at the end of days one or two? God was establishing a pattern: He makes good things; and light, the first thing that He made, was good. As mentioned above, the end-of-the-day evaluation component is missing in days one and two, not because God's initial creation was bad, but because it was still incomplete and not yet fit as a home for mankind.)

APPLICATION

A lesson about God's creative work should not only inspire discussion and God-honoring thoughts. It should inspire praise and thanksgiving: praise to God for His glory revealed in creation and thanksgiving for the fact that He created a beautiful home for mankind. Consider using Psalm 29 or Psalm 148 to sing praise to God for His work in Genesis 1. Psalm 29 emphasizes God's voice in conjunction with the creation. Psalm 148 encompasses the whole of creation and also speaks of God's commands in creation.

ACTIVITIES

1. The Nature of God. You can tell a lot about a person by what he does. Genesis 1 introduces us to God through His work in creation. Read through Genesis 1:1-13 and look for all the things God does. Make a list of God's actions below.

Unit 1: Creation and Fall

What do God's actions tell you about who He is?

2. The Purpose of Repetition. Read through Genesis 1:1-13 and find all the repeated words and phrases. Write them in the space below.

Pick two of the repeated words/phrases and write why you think they are repeated. What is the author trying to teach you or draw your attention to through the use of repetition?

3. Imagine the Beginning. Imagine what the earth might have looked like as God began His work of creation. Then draw four different pictures, one of each of the following.

(1) The earth when it was formless and empty

(2) The earth after God separated the waters above from the waters below

Unit 1: Creation and Fall

(3) The earth after God separated land from sea

(4) The earth after God commanded it to bring forth vegetation

4. Sing the Psalms. The story of creation should inspire praise in our hearts. The Psalms give us the words to praise God. Write a prayer of praise in response to Psalm 148 or Psalm 29 in the space below. _____
_____
_____
_____
_____

Lesson 1.1

EVALUATION

1. What did God do in this passage? Be specific.

2. What's repeated in the passage? Why do you think it is repeated?

3. What did God do in day three that He didn't do in days one and two? Why do you think that is?

4. What are the four aspects of God's creative activity?

5. What tools did God use to create?

6. What was the earth like before God began to form it?

LESSON 1.2

A Home for Mankind: God Filled the Heavens and the Earth

THE STORY

Lesson Theme - God filled the home He had created for mankind.

On days one through three, God built a home for mankind; and then on days four through six, He filled that home with furniture. But creation wasn't just meant to be a place for mankind to live, it was meant to be a domain for him to rule over. So God filled the creation with vegetation to adorn creation and provide sustenance for mankind, and then He filled it with life—creatures over which man was to exercise dominion.

In Genesis 1:3 "the earth was without form and void"; in other words, it had not been shaped into a meaningful form, and it was empty. Days four through six cycle back through what God had formed on days one through three with the days sequentially corresponding to each other. On day four, God filled what He had created on day one; on day five, God filled what He had created on day two; and on day six, God filled what He had created on day three.

God repeated the process of forming and filling with the creation of Adam, which is recorded in detail in Genesis 2. "And the LORD God formed man of the dust of the ground, and breathed into his nostrils the breath of life" (Gen 2:7). God formed man by dividing the dust from the ground and shaping it into the form of a man. Man was then filled with the life-giving breath of God. Likewise, when we believe in Jesus, we are

Formed (days 1-3) → Filled (days 4-6)

OVERVIEW

God formed the creation on days one through three; on days four through six, God filled creation, making it into a home for man. On day four, God created the heavenly lights to rule the day and night, give light to the earth and mark time (days, years and seasons). On day five, God filled the sea with sea creatures (fish and sea serpents), filled the sky with birds, and commanded them all to reproduce. On day six, God created the land animals (livestock, wild animals and creeping things). Finally, He created man (both male and female) to live in his well-prepared home which God now evaluated as very good.

SOURCE MATERIAL

- Genesis 1:14-31
- Psalm 8, 19 and 148
- Proverbs 24:4

formed into new creations and then filled with the Spirit.

Day four

On day four, God filled the heavens with lights; a lot of detail is given in Genesis 1:14-18 as to their purpose in creation. Notice that God didn't call them by their scientific names: neutron stars, red dwarfs or supergiants (not that there is anything wrong with these designations). God called them "lights," and one of their given purposes is to give light to the earth. Nothing in the creation

Unit 1: Creation and Fall

OBJECTIVES

Feel...

- awe at the glory of God that is revealed in the sky.
- gratitude for the perfectly suited environment that God made for man.

Understand...

- that in days three through six, God **filled** what He had **formed** in days one through three.
- that forming and filling is a pattern we will see repeated throughout the Bible.
- the purposes of the "lights" in creation: to give light, mark time, rule, and reveal God's glory.
- the categories of sea creatures: fish and great sea creatures (sea serpents).
- the categories of land animals in relation to man: livestock, wild animals, and creeping things.
- what God created on each of the seven days of creation.

Apply this understanding by...

- thanking God for forming a suitable home (earth) for you to live in.
- praising God for the beauty and majesty of the creation.

account is separated from the idea that God was making a *home* for man to live in, and every good home needs lights.

Additionally, every good home needs a clock and a calendar. The lights were given to serve as signs to mark seasons and days and years. The sun tells us when it's day (and even what time of day it is) and the moon tells us when it's night. Taken together, the heavenly lights indicate the seasons. The idea of "seasons" here is not winter, spring and fall, but specifically worship seasons; the heavenly lights would tell Israel when it was time to feast.

Another purpose given for the sun and the moon is to rule. The sun rules over the day; the moon rules over the night. God would create mankind on day six to rule over the earth, and in anticipation of man's dominion, God gave rulers to rule the sky. The sun exercises considerable authority over mankind; it tells us when to get up, when to go to bed, when to put on sunscreen, etc.... and it hurts when we don't obey!

The fourfold creation pattern continued in days four through six. On day four, God commanded the light into existence (Gen 1:14), then divided the day from night, just like He had separated the light from darkness on day one. He had named the light day and darkness night on day one, so He did not name on day four. However, God did evaluate His creation on day four (Gen 1:18).

Day five
In broad terms, creation can be broken down into the domains (1) sky, (2) sea and (3) land. God created living creatures to fill all three of these domains. On day five, God created the fish and the birds which fill the sea and sky. The sea and sky are the result of God separating the waters above from the waters below on day two. So on day five, we see God filling what He had formed on day two.

God created two categories of sea life on day five. First, fish: "let the waters abound with an abundance of living creatures" (Gen 1:20) and second, great sea creatures (Gen 1:21). The word translated as "great sea creatures" in Hebrew means dragon, or giant serpent (of which leviathan in Job 41 is an example). These creatures are now extinct, but in all likelihood, the serpent that deceived Eve in Genesis 3 was one of these creatures.

Day six
On day six, God filled the dry land He had divided from the waters on day three. God filled this dry ground with land animals and then created man to rule over creation.

The land animals are divided into three categories: (1) livestock, (2) wild animals and (3) creeping things. Notice that, as with the heavenly lights, the land animals were not named based on scientific categories. These biblical categories represent the animals in relationship to man, because God was creating a home for man, while science categorizes the animals based upon their relationships to one another.

In the final evaluation (Gen 1:31), God called the creation *very* good. This is because mankind, both man and woman for whom the creation was made, were now at home in it.

The whole process of creation reflects God's wisdom in preparing a suitable home for mankind.

APPLICATION

As in the previous lesson, continued reflection on God's creation should inspire praise and thanksgiving. Our God is a ridiculously generous giver. As an example of His generosity, consider a mark of a high quality and often expensive home in our culture: a high ceiling. And just think, we can't even see the ceiling on the home God has made for us! The sea, sky and land are overflowing with abundant life. Psalm 148 gives the ultimate purpose of all creation: to praise the Lord. This psalm is very appropriate for this lesson, because it moves through every category of creation, commanding them to praise the Lord.

ACTIVITIES

1. Word Lists. *This is an extension of the "Nature of God" and "Purpose of Repetition" activities from Lesson 1.1.* You can tell a lot about a person by what he does. Genesis 1 introduces us to God through His work in creation. Read through Genesis 1:14-31 and look for all the things God does. Make a list of the verbs below, thinking about what God's actions tell you about Him._____

_____

What verbs are in this list that weren't in Genesis 1:1-13? What do these verbs tell you about God?___

_____

_____

_____

Unit 1: Creation and Fall

Read through Genesis 1:14-31 and find all the repeated words and phrases. Write them in the space below._____

_____

Pick two of the repeated words/phrases and write why you think they are repeated; what is the author trying to teach you or draw your attention to through the use of repetition? (Pick different words/phrases from the ones you picked in the similar activity in Lesson 1.1.)_____

_____

_____

_____

2. In the Dark. God gave both light and darkness. Consider the following questions.

What are three ways we are restricted when we don't have light? _____

_____

_____

What are three ways light is helpful to us?_____

_____

_____

What is a way that darkness is good?_____

_____

_____

3. Food for Thought. God made the world as a perfectly suited home for mankind. For example, isn't it amazing that food we can actually eat grows on trees? After reading Psalm 8 and 148, write a prayer thanking God for how He has provided for us in the home He has made for us. _____

_____

_____

_____

_____

_____

EVALUATION

1. How were the second three days different from the first three days of creation? _____
_____
_____
_____

2. God did not call His creation good in days one and two, but then He did in day three and continued through day six. Why is this? _____
_____
_____

3. God called creation very good at the end of day six. Why did He do this at that time and not before?
_____
_____
_____

4. What did God create on day one? _____

   What did God create on day two? _____

   What did God create on day three? _____

   What did God create on day four? _____

   What did God create on day five? _____

   What did God create on day six? _____

5. What are the two categories of sea creatures? _____

   What are the three categories of land animals? _____

6. What do the heavens tells us? _____

7. What is the ultimate purpose of creation? _____
_____
_____
_____

LESSON 1.3

Kings and Queens of Creation: The Purpose of Mankind

UNIT 1

THE STORY

Lesson Theme - Mankind created as plural rulers in the image of God.

Mankind was created in God's image to be ruler over creation; Adam and Eve were meant to be the *perfect* king and queen over the *perfect* creation. When they ate the fruit of that forbidden tree, this royal calling is what they fell from. Ultimately, mankind will be restored to his place as perfect image-bearers ruling over creation—that is the hope of redemption.

Man was created in God's image. The deeper you dig into this truth, the more gems you'll find. Of course, the fact that we are created in the image of God accounts for all sorts of things: our ability to reason, communicate, explore and discover, make communities and have deep relationships. And that really just scratches the surface. We want to focus on just two things that are right on the surface in Genesis 1:26-30. First, being created in God's image means that as God is Trinitarian (plural), man is male and female (plural). Second, being created in God's image means that mankind is created to have dominion. God is sovereign over the whole universe, and if He is a ruler, His image must also be a ruler.

Man made in God's Trinitarian image
The word Trinity is not used in the Bible, but the fact that God is plural is not a theological invention, nor is it particularly difficult to discover. Notice the interesting use of singular and plural in Genesis 1:26*: "Then **God** *(sg)* said, 'Let **Us** *(pl)* make **man** *(sg)* in **Our** *(pl)* image, in **Our** *(pl)* likeness, and let **them** *(pl)* rule...'" It goes on like

OVERVIEW

God formed and filled the earth in the six days of creation. Finally, on the sixth day, He created mankind. God made man in His own image, which means that man is relational and plural (man and woman), and man is created to rule. The first thing God spoke to the man and the woman was a blessing and a commission: He told them to multiply, fill the earth and rule over it. God also provided food for man and animals alike. Finally, after six days of creation, God performed His last act of division: He set apart the seventh day as a day of rest for God and man alike.

SOURCE MATERIAL

- Genesis 1:26-2:3
- Psalm 8
- Proverbs 24:3

this all the way through the end of verse 27. God is referred to in both the singular and plural, and mankind is also spoken of in both the singular and the plural. Mankind being plural means that God designed man to have Trinitarian relationships with one another. (Marriage is the central image of a Trinitarian relationship—two becoming one flesh—but any number of relationships where people form relational ties that are more than the sum of their parts are examples of Trinitarian relationships). God could not create a singular male and have him be an accurate reflection of His multifaceted image. God is plural and diverse, so mankind had to be as well.

23

Unit 1: Creation and Fall

OBJECTIVES

Feel...

- honored and humbled that God would esteem you high enough to be an image-bearing king (or queen) in God's world (see Psalm 8).
- thankful that God has created you in His image.
- thankful that God has given man a day of rest.

Understand...

- that man is created in the image of God.
  - This means that there are both male and female, and they are created as relational beings.
  - This means that mankind is created to rule.
- that the first command God gave man was to be fruitful (reproduce) and rule over the earth.
- that God provided for the needs of man and the animals. (God provided vegetation and fruit.)

Apply this understanding by...

- considering what areas of responsibility God has given you and evaluating how you are ruling in those areas.
- thanking God for the ways He has provided for you.

Made to rule
God then blessed and commissioned His image-bearers to rule over creation (Gen 1:28). If you ask someone what the first thing God said to Adam and Eve was, you're likely to hear something like, "Don't eat from the tree of the knowledge of good and evil." Most people think the first thing God said was prohibition. Actually, the first thing God said was a spoken blessing: be fruitful and multiply—make babies! Then God gave them responsibility—told them to rule over the earth. What a blessing! God is not a killjoy. He's not, fundamentally, a rule-maker. God loves to bless and that's the first thing He did after making Adam and Eve.

God told Adam and Eve to have dominion over the whole earth: land, sea, sky and the creatures in them (Gen 1:29-31). But also notice that the lights were left out of man's dominion. The purpose of the lights is to reveal the glory of God and, therefore, are not within man's domain.

However, within the domain God has entrusted to man, this command ultimately encompasses every earthly task imaginable. By implication, man was commissioned here to build roads, cities, cultivate the ground, farm animals and create culture and civilization. We often think of these endeavors as secular extras and not real service to God. However, doing these things is actually being obedient to God's first command to mankind and in keeping with man's purpose.

Notice also that God provided for His creation. He gave vegetation on the earth for the sustenance of both man and animals. God called man to the high task of ruling the earth, but gave him the life he needed to engage this task.

The Sabbath
The man's first full day was God's seventh; the man and woman started out with rest. God has created us to need and enjoy one day of rest out of every seven. What a blessing that God did not just say, "Get to work," but started man and woman off with worship and rest. God set apart or divided the seventh day as holy from the other six; this is a continuation of the theme of division.

APPLICATION

The application to this lesson is simple, but very important: God created us to take dominion over creation. The questions you want to wrestle with on this point are: What all does dominion entail? What am I currently being called to rule over? What am I currently doing that falls into the category of dominion that I may not even be recognizing as such?

We live in a secularized culture and have bought the lie that there is such a thing as secular work. But nothing is secular that is commanded by God. This means that our learning, even in math, English and technology is right at the heart of what God created and commanded us to do. Working hard at your studies is faithful obedience, just like loving your neighbor or praying.

ACTIVITIES

1. The Trinity Reflected in Mankind. Work through Genesis 1:26-27* (below) and mark all the personal nouns and pronouns (in bold) as either singular or plural in the parentheses.

Then **God** ( ) said, "Let **Us** ( ) make **man** ( ) in **Our** ( ) image, in **Our** ( ) likeness, and let **them** ( ) rule... So **God** ( ) created **man** ( ); in **His** ( ) own image, in the image of **God** ( ) **He** ( ) created **him** ( ); **male and female** ( ) He ( ) created **them** ( ).

What do you observe from this activity? _____
_____
_____
_____

What do the observations tell you about the nature of God and mankind? _____
_____
_____
_____
_____

Unit 1: Creation and Fall

2. Imagine: Life Without the Fall. In the space below, write a short paragraph, imagining what the world may have been like in the years and centuries after Adam and Eve were created had they not eaten from the tree of the knowledge of good and evil. _____

_____
_____
_____
_____
_____
_____
_____
_____
_____
_____
_____

List at least three different jobs people can do that are not considered "religious work" (like a missionary or pastor), but are still true obedience to God's command to subdue the earth. _____

_____
_____
_____

3. Read Psalm 8 and then write a prayer below in response to the truth that God has given mankind dominion over all creation._____

_____
_____
_____
_____
_____
_____

Lesson 1.3

EVALUATION

1. What does it mean that mankind was created in God's image? _____
_____

2. What was the first command given to mankind? _____
_____

3. What was excluded from man's domain? _____
_____

4. What did God give mankind for food? _____
_____

5. What was man's responsibility on his first full day? _____
_____

The Garden as a Tabernacle

Diagram of the Garden

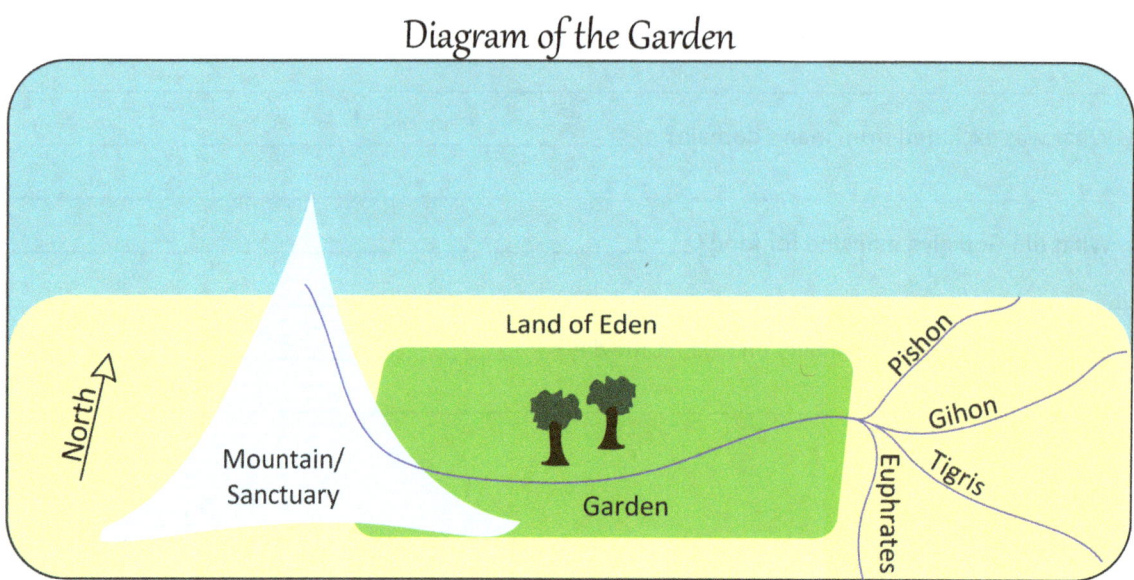

For Comparison: Israel's Tabernacle

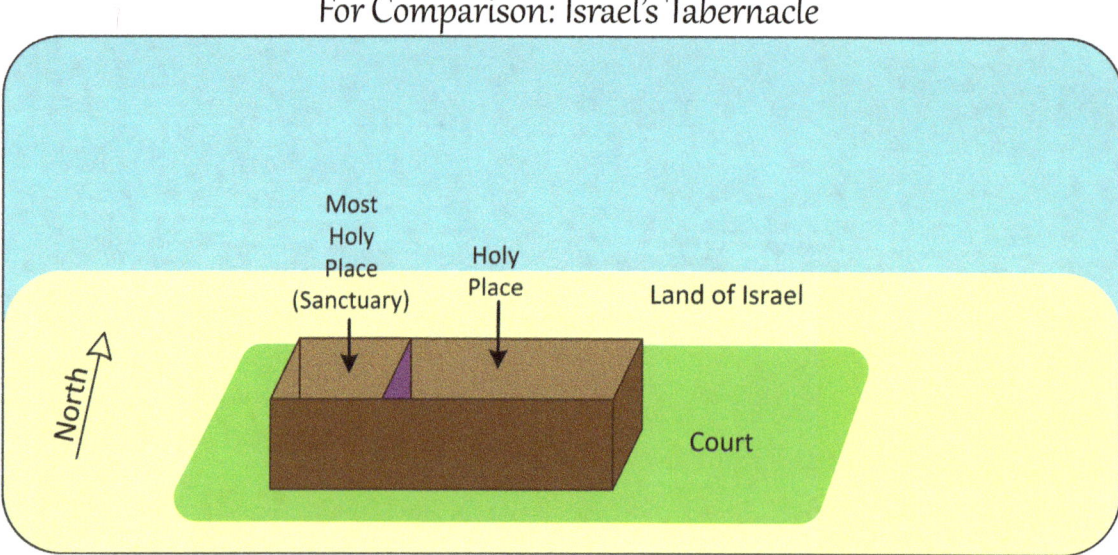

LESSON 1.4

Training Ground: The Man as Priest and Protector of the Garden

UNIT 1

THE STORY

Lesson Theme - Adam as the priest of the garden
God created Adam and put him in the garden. We know from Genesis 1:26-30 that mankind's purpose on the earth was to rule over it, but for now, his domain was limited to the garden. The garden was his training ground. The language used of Adam's responsibilities in the garden points to his role as a priest—he was to tend and keep the garden. When God later instituted worship in the tabernacle, this same language—to tend and to keep—was used to describe the responsibilities of the priests.

There are three character types that play a central role throughout the Old Testament: priests, kings and prophets. The books of Moses are primarily about priests. The books of history and the writings are primarily about kings. The books of the prophets are, well, about prophets.

Priests are, in many ways, like children. They are given direct orders and told to simply obey. They aren't often called to deep wisdom and aren't called into God's council—to advise Him. Kings, on the other hand, are called to go beyond simple obedience and have a responsibility to make judgments using principles of wisdom. Prophets, finally, are called into God's council; they hear directly from God and even advise God (much like Abraham did when God was considering destroying Sodom and Gomorrah).

The garden as a sanctuary
The garden was a place of perfection: Adam and Eve lived there naked, so it was warm, but not

OVERVIEW

Having seen how God established man's home in the world and designed man and woman as the king and queen of the earth, we now zoom in on day six of the story. God made a garden, a perfect environment where man could learn his responsibilities to God and to the world in which he lived; then God gave the man work to do and commands to obey.

SOURCE MATERIAL

- Genesis 2:4-17
- Ezekiel 28:11-15
- Psalms 8, 104
- Proverbs 1:8, 30:17

too warm, with soft grass and lots of food to eat and water to drink. God brought a mist to water the plants, so there was no need to haul around a watering can. Adam and Eve didn't have to cook; they could just pick fruit off the trees.

But the garden was more than just a comfortable place to live. By connecting the dots between Genesis 2:4-17 and Ezekiel 28:11-15, we gain a fuller picture of the garden as a place of worship, a sanctuary. The Ezekiel passage describes an angel (a cherub, perhaps Lucifer) who lived in Eden, on God's mountain sanctuary. Often, Eden gets equated with the garden, as though Eden is the name of the garden. Actually, the garden is said to be on the east side of the land of Eden (a region rather than a specific place—Gen 2:8). The

Unit 1: Creation and Fall

OBJECTIVES

Feel...

- gratitude to God for providing a place where all man's needs are provided for.
- a longing for and disconnect with the world of the garden (since it's the world we lost).

Understand...

- that man is made of dust and breath.
- the layout of the garden as man's perfect home and God's dwelling place.
- the names of the two trees and which one was forbidden.
- Adam's responsibility to tend and keep the garden.

Apply this understanding by...

- identifying your own areas of responsibility.
- evaluating your performance in those areas.
- celebrating where you are already succeeding.
- identifying positive changes he can make that will lead to further success.

mountain of God (Ezek 28:14) is also in Eden. We know from Genesis 2 that a river flowed out of the garden and watered the whole region. Since water flows downhill, we can be sure that the river began in the sanctuary (mountain), flowed down into the garden and thence to the world. Putting this all together, Eden was a region with a garden on the east and a mountain just to the west of this garden.

The creation of Adam

In Genesis 1, we find an overview of the seven days of creation. Genesis 2:4-25 retells the story of day six (the day mankind was created) in greater detail. Adam was made from dust. God **formed** the man from the dust of the ground and breathed life into him (**filled** him with breath/life).

There are a couple of observations to take away from this. First, observe the fact that God repeated the pattern of forming and filling here in the creation of man. Second, we have an indication of what man was made of. Dust formed the body of man; breath formed his spirit (spirit and breath are the same word in Hebrew). When the body and spirit were united together, man became a "living being" (Gen 2:7). The word behind "living being" is the closest word Hebrew has for soul. Therefore, Dust + Breath= Living Being or Body + Spirit = Soul. Genesis 2:7 is the foundational passage for anything related to body, spirit or soul in the Bible. When we die, our body and spirit are separated; when we are resurrected, our body and spirit are reunited, and we again become complete persons.

Adam's priestly responsibilities

So Adam lived in this perfect garden sanctuary and was there to tend and to keep it (Gen 2:15). To tend the garden meant to cultivate, or care for the vegetation. The garden was a beautiful and glorious place, but there was still work to be done and further duties related to the care and glorification of the garden. To keep the garden meant to protect it from external harm: intruders and enemies. So Adam's job was to serve dutifully within the garden and protect the garden from anything outside that might seek to harm it or its inhabitants. As we noted above, these were priestly duties, the same kinds of things that would later be required of the priests in the tabernacle.

Next we see a simple priestly command for Adam to obey. "And the LORD God commanded the man, saying, 'Of every tree of the garden you may freely eat; but of the tree of the knowledge of good and evil you shall not eat, for in the day that you eat of it you shall surely die'" (Gen 2:16-17). The tree of the knowledge of good and evil as well as the tree of life were right in the midst of the garden and probably had significance regarding the worship of the Lord. There was nothing innately wicked about the tree of the knowledge of good and evil; it was a good creation of God. Perhaps, one day, God would allow Adam to eat from this tree; but for now, tasting its fruit was forbidden. This was the only prohibition that God gave to Adam.

APPLICATION

God was Adam's father; He loved him and gave him a beautiful place to live. He had also given Adam's life meaning—he was a priest in God's holy dwelling place and had certain responsibilities that went along with his role; he was to tend and to keep the garden. God has given all of us provision and responsibility as well. Think through all the ways God has blessed you with provision and what responsibilities you have. What is your garden "to tend and to keep"?

ACTIVITIES

1. Imagination: Drawing the Garden. Draw the garden of Eden with the tree of life and the tree of knowledge of good and evil.

Unit 1: Creation and Fall

2. Imagination: Honoring Parents. Represent the following Proverb in a drawing:

"The eye that mocks his father, and scorns obedience to his mother, the ravens of the valley will pick it out, and the young eagles will eat it" (Proverbs 30:17).

3. Celebration. The story of creation should inspire praise in our hearts. The Psalms give us the words to praise God. Write a prayer of praise in response to Psalm 104 in the space below. _____

_____
_____
_____
_____

4. Journal Time. Reflect on God's blessing on Adam and Eve in the garden and think about the work God has called you to do and all the ways He has provided for you. Write a paragraph in the space below listing some of the ways God has provided for you and some of the jobs He has called you to do. Think about the following questions as you write: Has God provided everything you need? Has God given a job for you to do in your life? What do you need to "tend and keep"? Spend some time praying and thanking God and asking for His help in your tasks._____

_____
_____
_____
_____
_____
_____

Lesson 1.4

EVALUATION

1. What is man made of? _____

2. Label the diagram below with the following words/phrases: *Garden, Sanctuary, Land of Eden*

3. What were the names of the two trees?_____
_____

4. Which tree *could* Adam and Eve eat from? _____
_____

5. What was man's job in the garden? _____
_____

6. What does it mean to guard something? _____
_____

7. What do you think man was supposed to guard the garden from? _____
_____

8. Did man have everything he needed in the garden? Make a list._____
_____
_____

LESSON 1.5

The King's Companion: The Creation of Woman

UNIT 1

THE STORY

Lesson Theme - A helper suitable for man
It follows naturally from the fact that mankind was created in the image of God, that a singular male simply doesn't fit the bill. God is three in one and one in three; therefore, a creation in His image must be plural, capable of coming together in perfect unity. In Genesis 2:18-25, we witness the creation of the woman, a perfectly suitable match and helper for Adam. Adam needed a woman—for companionship, to aid in his duties as priest, and ultimately, as a counterpart in his calling to take dominion over all the earth.

Not good for man to be alone
Only once in the creation account did God say that something was *not* good (Gen 2:18). This is a major point of departure. *Why* was it not good for man to be alone? God made man to be His image. You might describe it as God looking in a mirror and painting a self-portrait in the creation. When God looks in the mirror, He does not see a single Person; He is one God in three Persons. God is a community, and there is no community in one man, so God made a helper for man. Not to mention that the task God gave in Genesis 1:27-28 could not possibly have been accomplished without the help of a counterpart.

So God decided that since it was not good for man to be alone, He would make an appropriate counterpart for him. But instead of telling Adam about his need for a helper, God let Adam discover it himself. God brought the animals to Adam for him to name (Gen 2:19-20). Apparently, Adam was aware that he was lacking something, because he looked for a suitable counterpart from among the animals and didn't find one.

God built a woman
God's method of creating the woman is significant and calls us back to the fact that God created mankind in His image. God is one and three; in order to make a proper reflection of His image, the woman *had* to come out of the man—she had to be one with him from the very beginning.

So God put Adam to sleep (Gen 2:21), which was a death of sorts for Adam. After Adam went to sleep, God cut his side and removed a rib.

OVERVIEW

God intended mankind to be His image and accordingly gave mankind the tasks of protecting and governing the world, but these were not jobs a single man could do by himself. God took Adam through an exercise where Adam came to understand that he needed a helper, and then God provided him with a helper suitable for him in every way.

SOURCE MATERIAL

- Genesis 2:18-25
- Psalm 128
- Proverbs 18:22

Unit 1: Creation and Fall

OBJECTIVES

Feel...

- initial puzzlement at why God chose to create man and woman in stages.
- awe at how many people we need.

Understand...

- why Adam wasn't an accurate reflection of God's image without a helper.
- why Adam needed Eve to fulfill their calling.
- how Eve was supposed to be a helper for Adam.
- that Adam and Eve were originally one—she was made from his flesh and bones, and they would again be made one in marriage.
- that, even today, the story of Eve's creation is the foundation for marriage.

Apply this understanding by...

- recognizing that you too need other people.
- thanking God for providing the people you depend upon.

Interestingly, the word used in Hebrew for the creation of woman is not the common word meaning "make," which is used often in the creation narrative. Instead, it is a more specific word meaning "build" and is used in the Bible when referring to the building of a city or temple. This use of the word "build" to refer to the creation of woman seems odd, and it is a little bit. Likewise, one day, the second Adam would die, His side would be pierced, and the Church, His body, would be built as an everlasting dwelling place for God in the Spirit.

The institution of marriage
When Adam awoke and was introduced to Eve, he immediately recognized what had happened; God had made woman from his very own flesh and bone (Gen 2:23). Not only that, but Adam also understood that since the woman came out of him, the two of them were meant to be one. This was the marriage of Adam and Eve. Genesis 2:24 is important: marriage *now* is the way it is because God made man and woman (and marriage) in the way that He did. The Creator has the right to define how marriage works—and thousands of years later, it still works that way.

Adam and Eve began their earthly lives naked and at peace in the garden. They were like children, not yet bearing the glory of righteousness, but neither were they guilty. They were free from the shame and darkness that the fall would bring in to the world in just a short period of time. They had nothing to hide.

APPLICATION

In our culture, a helper sounds like a housekeeper or servant, but the connotation of the word used in Genesis 2 is much more significant than that. Often in the Bible, God Himself is called a helper; and more specifically, the Holy Spirit is called a helper in the New Testament. A helper wasn't just a nice bonus for Adam. Without the woman, Adam wasn't himself and couldn't accurately reflect God's image, nor was he even able to come close to accomplishing his purpose. This should go without saying, but we'll say it anyway: woman was created in God's image just as much as the man was.

Beyond this, without the woman, there would be no sons and daughters, no multiplication; it would be extremely difficult, if not impossible, to make daily life and dominion happen on this earth without numerous people. Your life is made possible my many "helpers," and this means you need to be thankful to God for all He has provided.

ACTIVITIES

1. Psalm 128 give us God's perspective on the joy and value of family. Specifically, it says that a wife "is like a fruitful vine" and children are "like olive plants". How does this relate to what you have learned in this lesson? _____

_____

_____

_____

_____

What does fruitfulness look like in the context of family relationships? Give three specific examples.___

_____

_____

_____

_____

_____

_____

Unit 1: Creation and Fall

2. All Our Helpers. Adam needed Eve in order to do the work God gave him to do (Genesis 1:27-28). List all the people you need in order to do the things God gives you to do. _____

_____
_____
_____
_____
_____
_____
_____
_____
_____
_____

2. Journal Time and Challenge: Giving Thanks. After tracing back all the helpers we need for daily life, spend some time writing in the space below, giving thanks to God for all the help He has provided for you._____

_____
_____
_____
_____
_____
_____
_____
_____
_____
_____

Then, think of someone who has helped you and thank them this week. Write their name below.

_____

EVALUATION

1. God made man from dust and breath. What did God make woman from? _____
_____

2. How did the man recognize the woman? _____
_____

3. What did God tell Adam to do? _____
_____
_____

4. Why did Adam need Eve? _____
_____
_____

5. What did God say was "not good"? _____
_____

6. How does God's creation of both man and woman reflect the Trinity? _____
_____
_____
_____

7. What does the creation of Eve have to do with marriage today? _____
_____
_____
_____

LESSON 1.6

The Serpent's Attack: The Temptation of Eve and the Failure of the King

THE STORY

Lesson Theme - The serpent tempted Eve by lying about God.

God had given Adam, and with him Eve, authority over all of creation. The serpent approached Eve in order to redirect her; he wanted to move her away from gratitude and love for her generous Creator and turn her and her husband to disobedience. Adam and Eve's disobedience would put the serpent in a position of assumed authority over them (you become a slave of the one you obey) and thus, over all creation.

The few verses at the beginning of Genesis 3 contain a great amount of significant information, and most of that is in between and underneath the words on the page. On the surface, the serpent's words were simple, but they were incredibly subversive. The serpent's aim was to undermine God's goodness and authority over Adam and Eve.

The serpent and the temptation

The serpent was a cunning animal, but he was still an animal (Gen 3:1). Of course, we know there was more to him: the serpent was a manifestation of Satan, a fallen angel. While this is true and will come out with great clarity later on in the Story, in order to tell this story the way God tells it, it's best to stick closely to the text on this point: the serpent was an animal. Therefore, the serpent was (1) under the dominion of man and (2) lower on the created order than man. Immediately jumping to talk of fallen angels sidesteps both of these important points.

OVERVIEW

God established creation as a home for man to rule over. He planted a garden in which man would function as a priest and receive training as a king, and He gave man a woman as a helper and companion to fulfill his God-given task on the earth. Now, God tested the man and the woman. The serpent deceived the woman, and she ate from the tree God had forbidden them to eat from; Adam willfully sinned and also ate from the tree. The man and the woman now knew good and evil and had given the serpent their authority over creation.

SOURCE MATERIAL

- Genesis 3:1-6
- Psalm 119:153-160 (especially verse 160)
- Proverbs 27:20
- 1 John 2:16

The serpent began his attack by simply asking a question, *but* it was not *just* a question. "Has God really said, 'You may not eat from any tree in the garden'?" (Gen 3:1*). The question is absurd on its face. God, in fact, said the opposite; not just every tree in the garden, but every fruit bearing tree on earth was given to man for food (Gen 1:29). But imagine the seed of mistrust this question placed in Eve's mind. What kind of God would make a home for man and then prohibit him from eating from *any* tree? *And*, if it would have been stingy for God to prohibit all trees,

Unit 1: Creation and Fall

OBJECTIVES

Feel...

- a sense of the power of the serpent's manipulative deception.
- spite toward the serpent for how he deceived Eve.
- frustration as he watches Eve walk right into the serpent's trap.
- frustration towards Adam for not manning up and protecting the garden and the woman.

Understand...

- how the serpent tempted the woman:
  - by getting her to question God's goodness (and thus undermining her ability to be thankful).
  - by getting her to question God's ability to speak authoritatively.
- that Adam didn't do his job of protecting the garden and his wife.
- that Adam gave his authority over creation to the serpent (as *de facto* ruler of creation).

Apply this understanding by...

- determining areas of your life where you are not being grateful.
- contemplating how a lack of gratitude opens you up to temptations to sin.
- thanking God for the things you have not been thankful for.

isn't it a bit stingy for God to prohibit even one tree? In this way, the serpent was calling into question whether God was really being generous in providing for man's sustenance and making a good home for man.

Adam and Eve should have been so thankful for everything God had given them that the temptation to doubt His goodness would seem absolutely absurd to them. God had given them a paradise, a garden with life-sustaining food that grew on trees and life-giving water that flowed throughout. Notice how the serpent's question, when taken seriously, redirected Eve from gratitude towards God to questioning God's goodness.

The serpent's simple lead-in here, "Has God really said..." has some important ramifications as well. The serpent was calling into question God's ability to authoritatively speak. The serpent was attacking the very center of God's sovereignty as Creator (God speaks and it is so). The serpent did not need the woman to actually change her mind about what God had said, but only to make her believe that she had the authority to make judgement regarding God and His spoken word.

Eve could have given at least a couple of appropriate responses to the serpent's question. First and probably best, would have been to say, "Hey God, this serpent says You're stingy; is that true?" After all, God lived right there with them; there is no reason to think that He wouldn't have come running to help them with temptation in their time of need. Another valid option would have been to stand in gratitude and respond boldly, "That is an absurd question. Of course God has not prohibited us from eating from any tree; He is a good and generous God." Instead, the woman took the bait. In effect she said, "No, God didn't say we couldn't eat from any tree; but, now that you mention it, He did say we couldn't eat from the tree in the middle of the garden or we would die. What's up with God doing that?"

In Genesis 3:4-5, the serpent then responded with an outright lie mixed with a little truth (for all lies must have a little truth in them to be believable at all). He denied that they would die, which was a lie. He also said they would be like God, knowing good and evil, and this part was true (see Gen 3:22). The tree of the knowledge of good and evil had been a sort of test for Adam and Eve. Had they passed the test, they would have known good and evil by overcoming evil with good. Instead, they came to know good and evil by failure.

Now, having believed the lie that maybe God didn't have their best interest in mind and believing the lie that she wouldn't die if she ate it, the woman took a look at the fruit. She saw that it was (1) good for food (which was true), (2) pleasing to the eye (which was true) and (3) desirable to make one wise (which was false—God had told her that it brought death, not wisdom; the serpent had deceived her into believing this subtle lie about the tree). These are the three ways in which humans are always tempted. The fruit was "good for food," or appealing to the flesh (lust of the flesh); it was "pleasant to the eyes" (lust of the eyes); and it was "desirable to make one wise," an appeal to the quest for human greatness (boastful pride of life) (Gen 3:6a).

Adam ceded his authority over creation
Eve then gave some fruit to her husband and he ate (Gen 3:6b). It is worth making a few comments regarding Adam at this point. His job in the garden was to tend and keep (cultivate and guard) it. He was near enough to Eve for her to simply give him some fruit. There is a good chance he was present during the serpent's conversation with the woman. He should have stopped the serpent, shut him up or crushed his head, but he failed his training; he did not guard the garden and protect his wife.

Instead of being king and queen over creation, Adam and Eve submitted to creation and gave the serpent authority over it and over them. The serpent was now ruler over this world, not by divine decree, but because the ruler over the world (man) had given his authority to the serpent. Man is still called to have dominion over creation; but, until the serpent is conquered, man will always have an enemy attempting to subvert his dominion activity.

APPLICATION

There are lots of things you can do as a Christian to protect yourself from temptation, but we want to focus in on two of the most important. First, cultivate an attitude of constant gratitude toward our generous Father. Had Adam and Eve done this, the serpent's subtle hints that God was a bit stingy would have seemed absurd. When we are tempted, the same tactic is almost always used: "God has been holding out on you, there is a good thing that He didn't want you to have." The practice of gratitude can protect us from this subtle lie.

Second, Eve could have simply asked God about what the serpent was saying. Likewise, if we develop a constant conversational relationship with the Lord, asking God what He thinks about our temptations will be the most natural thing in the world.

Unit 1: Creation and Fall

ACTIVITIES

1. Adam and Eve's Bible. Read back through Genesis 1-2 (starting in 1:26) and write a list of everything God told the man and the woman. _____

_____

_____

_____

What, if anything did Eve hear directly from God? _____

_____

_____

How did Eve know what she told the serpent in Genesis 3:2-3? _____

_____

_____

From your list above (Adam and Eve's Bible, everything they had heard from God), which things had they ignored, disbelieved or disobeyed in Genesis 3? List these things below. _____

_____

_____

_____

_____

What should Adam and Eve have done about the things God told them? _____

_____

2. What are the Idols? God is the only one who authoritatively speaks the truth (speaks and it is), He is the only Creator and Sustainer of life. When Adam and Eve stopped looking to God as the truth and life-giver, they necessarily replaced Him with an Idol. What idols did Adam and Eve worship instead of God in Genesis 3:1-6? _____

_____

_____

3. Draw It. Using stick figures, draw a picture of what was happening when the serpent deceived Eve. Where is Adam in your picture? Where is God in your picture?

Unit 1: Creation and Fall

4. Journal Time: Gratitude. Spend some time evaluating your own life and answering the questions below.

What are some areas in your life where God has provided for you abundantly, but you have not been thankful? _____

_____

_____

_____

_____

_____

_____

What temptations will (or has) your lack of gratitude led to? _____

_____

_____

_____

_____

5. Read Psalm 119:160 then write your own prayer of praise for the fact that God's truth an His righteous judgments are always and forever true._____

_____

_____

_____

_____

_____

_____

Lesson 1.6

EVALUATION

1. What are two truths about God the serpent was working to undermine when he spoke to Eve? _____

2. When the serpent first approached Eve, did he directly lie to her? _____

3. What was Adam doing during the serpent's conversation with Eve? _____
_____

4. What was Adam's responsibility in this situation? _____
_____

5. What did it cost Adam when he submitted to the serpent? _____
_____

6. What should have been Adam and Eve's response to God's provision? _____
_____

LESSON 1.7

Relationships Broken Between the King, His Companion and Their God

THE STORY

Lesson Theme - Adam and Eve's sin broke relationships.

When Adam and Eve sinned by eating from the tree of the knowledge of good and evil, serious damage was done in a number of different ways. Perhaps most significantly, their sin broke relationships, first with one another and then with God. God created Adam and Eve to reflect His image, but now they hid from each other (by making fig leaf coverings), and then they hid from God among the trees in the garden. (Sin makes you foolish enough to believe you can hide from God.) Hiding is a manifestation of broken relationships.

Background

God had told Adam and Eve that in the day that they ate from the fruit of the tree of the knowledge of good and evil they would surely die (Gen 2:17), but notice that they did not drop dead physically that day. So what did God mean when He told them they would die? Perhaps a better question would be, "What is death?" Death is when united Trinitarian relationships are severed. Physical death is when a person's spirit (breath) is separated from his body (dust). The death God was referring to was deeper than physical death; it was a severing of the Trinitarian unity between Adam and Eve and between them and God.

Sin always comes back to bite us; sometimes the consequences are what we might call formal, but there are always natural consequences to sin. Formal consequences are officially enforced disciplinary measures from someone in author-

OVERVIEW

Adam and Eve had eaten of the fruit of the tree of the knowledge of good and evil. God had told them that in the day they did this, they would surely die. After eating of the tree, Adam and Eve hid from each other because they were ashamed of their nakedness; their relationship was broken. Then, they attempted to hide from God in the garden. They were filled with fear, shame, and folly. When God approached them, Adam blamed Eve and *God*, and Eve blamed the serpent.

SOURCE MATERIAL

- Genesis 3:7-13
- Psalm 55
- Proverbs 16:10

ity; natural consequences are the ones that we experience whether anyone knows of our sin or not—fear, guilt and shame, for example. For kids, the formal consequences of sin often eclipse the natural consequences. But it is important as children grow into young adults that they learn to "read" natural consequences in their own lives. When they grow up, they won't get grounded when they sin; many times there will only be the natural consequences: broken relationships, fear and shame (the same things we see Adam and Eve experience in these verses).

They hid

The first thing that happened after Adam and Eve had eaten from the tree of the knowledge of

Unit 1: Creation and Fall

OBJECTIVES

Feel...

- the pain of the broken relationships caused by Adam and Eve's sin.
- a connection of common experience with Adam and Eve; everyone knows what it feels like to be betrayed by sin.
- a sense of loss regarding what Adam and Eve gave up when they sinned: their status as glorious king and queen and the peace and innocence of garden life.
- hope in the coming restoration.

Understand...

- the meaning of natural consequences of sin.
- the natural consequences of sin in this passage: broken relationships, loss of status, fear, shame and foolish thought.
- that Adam betrayed both Eve and God and blamed others when approached by God.

Apply this understanding by...

- identifying any areas where you have betrayed or been betrayed by a friend or family member.
- praying for God to bring restoration to these relationships.

good and evil was that their eyes were opened (Gen 3:7). This was not a good thing—they now knew evil, because they had committed it. The first thing Adam and Eve experienced with their new knowledge of good and evil was an awareness that they were naked: they experienced shame. Immediately, they sought to hide from each other, so they made coverings out of fig leaves.

After first hiding from each other, Adam and Eve heard God walking in the garden and hid from Him. Just like they had hid their nakedness from each other behind fig leaves, so they now hid from God behind leaves; they "hid themselves from the presence of the LORD God among the trees of the garden" (Gen 3:8).

God asked Adam where he was, and in response, Adam admitted that he "was afraid because [he] was naked, so [he] hid" (Gen 3:10). Sin causes fear. One of the lies the enemy wants us to believe is that sin is freedom, when actually, the opposite is true. Sin leads to bondage and bondage to fear and shame. Adam was no longer acting like a king. He was created to rule over the garden and ultimately the world, but his sin had taken away his ability to act as king. He now ran away and hid.

Then God pushed Adam further: "Who told you that you were naked? Have you eaten from the tree of which I commanded you that you should not eat?" (Gen 3:11). In response, Adam blamed Eve and God. Notice Adam's response to God, "The woman whom *You* gave to be with me, she gave me of the tree, and I ate" (Gen 3:12, emphasis added). In other words, "It's really Your fault, God; You gave me the woman who caused all this." Most of Adam's statement is patently false. One of his most important duties as priest in the garden was to protect it and its inhabitants. Had Adam done his job, it is likely that the woman would have never eaten the fruit.

Contrary to what Adam said, it wasn't God and the woman who betrayed him. Adam betrayed both himself and the woman. Adam intentionally let the woman fall into sin and failed in the calling that God had given him. The serpent was the only one with more culpability than Adam.

APPLICATION

Sin really does lead to shame, fear and broken relationships. But we can be confident that our wise and gracious God forgives, heals and redeems us of all our sin. Spend some time reflecting on a time when you sinned and experienced the kinds of natural consequences Adam and Eve experienced in Genesis 3. If you are still bearing a burden of guilt and shame, you have the glorious opportunity to experience God's forgiveness and healing. Confess your sin and let God's abundant favor wash over you.

ACTIVITIES

1. Sin's Consequences. Think about a time that you sinned and experienced both formal consequences and natural consequences.

Which consequences were worse, the formal or natural? Explain. _____
_____
_____
_____

Which consequences lasted longer? _____
_____
_____

In the past, which were you more likely to think of when you were tempted, the formal or the natural consequences? _____
_____

Now that you've seen how the consequences worked out for Adam and Eve which will you think more about in the future: the natural or formal consequences? Explain. _____
_____
_____
_____

Unit 1: Creation and Fall

2. Betrayal and Psalm 55. Identify a person who has betrayed you (lied to you, abandoned you for another friend, stabbed you in the back, stopped talking to you). In the space below, briefly describe the circumstance and how you felt (or still feel) about it. _____

_____

_____

_____

_____

_____

Now, connect your experience of betrayal to what Adam did to Eve and God. In what ways was what Adam did similar to your experience? _____

_____

_____

_____

_____

Read Psalm 55 (especially verses 12-22), imagining this psalm describing both Adam's betrayal and the betrayal you experienced. Then do as the psalmist says and "Cast your burden on the LORD" (Ps 55:22). Write a prayer to God, "casting" your experience with betrayal upon Him._____

_____

_____

_____

_____

_____

_____

_____

Lesson 1.7

EVALUATION

1. What are formal consequences for sin? What are natural consequences? _____
_____
_____
_____
_____

2. What natural consequences happen in this passage? _____
_____
_____
_____

3. Whom did Adam blame when God asked him if he ate from the tree? _____
_____
_____

4. Was it right for Adam and Eve to be afraid of God? _____
_____
_____
_____
_____
_____

5. God said that Adam and Eve would die in the day they ate from the fruit of the tree of the knowledge of good and evil. Did they die? What kind of death? _____
_____
_____
_____
_____
_____

LESSON 1.8

The Hope of Restoration: The Seed Will Crush the Serpent's Head

THE STORY

Lesson Theme - Deliverance promised through the enemy's defeat

After disobeying God and eating from the tree of the knowledge of good and evil, Adam and Eve lived in a fundamentally broken world. Their relationship with God was broken, their relationship with each other was broken, and creation itself groaned under the weight of their sin. But hope was not lost. God promised in Genesis 3:14-15 that the enemy would be defeated, his head would be crushed, and through his defeat the world would be redeemed. This passage is the foundation to the thematic center of the biblical Story. The concepts in this passage will be revisited many times throughout the Bible.

The serpent is the antagonist

The serpent is the bad guy in the story of Adam and Eve. People often think of Adam and Eve as the antagonists of the story (and they were certainly culpable). Ultimately though, mankind would be redeemed; the serpent was going to get his head crushed and end up in the lake of fire. In fact, it is through the serpent's defeat that mankind would be redeemed.

So, since the serpent is the enemy, God addressed him first. Adam and Eve would both be disciplined by God in the following verses—there were real consequences to their sin. But the serpent was *cursed*. From that day forward, the mighty serpent would get around on his belly and eat dust, a foreshadowing of the final defeat of the serpent when Jesus crushed his head on the cross. This is a signpost of redemption built into creation; whenever you see a serpent crawl-

OVERVIEW

Now that the man and woman had sinned and given up their authority over creation to the serpent, God set into motion the process of redemption (a process that would take millennia). The redemption would come by means of a descendant of the woman (the Messiah) crushing the head of the serpent. Once the serpent was defeated, mankind would be returned to his rightful place as ruler over creation. This passage is the background to many head-crushings of many serpent-people throughout the Bible.

SOURCE MATERIAL

- Genesis 3:14-15
- Psalms 8 and 91
- Proverbs 28:10

ing on its belly, it is a message that Satan will be defeated.

The serpent's curse contrasts sharply with the serpent's position as de-facto ruler of creation. When Adam obeyed the serpent, Adam, as ruler of the world, ceded his reign to the serpent, who was promptly cursed in greater measure than all of creation.

The woman and the seed

In Genesis 3:15, God addressed the serpent and said, "I will put enmity between you and the woman, and between your seed and hers." There are several layers of meaning here. First of all,

Unit 1: Creation and Fall

OBJECTIVES

Feel...

- a certain godly spite toward the serpent and Satan as the antagonist of the Story.
- gratitude toward God for promising the ultimate defeat of the serpent so early in the Story.
- excitement about the coming Story as a head-crushing battle between good and evil.

Understand...

- that the serpent was the bad guy (even though Adam and Eve were culpable).
- that the serpent was cursed to belly-crawling as a foreshadowing of the ultimate defeat of evil.
- that the seed of the serpent is anyone who follows the serpent.
- that the seed of the woman is first and foremost the Messiah, but also anyone who is a type or picture of the Messiah.
- that the serpent would ultimately be defeated by head-crushing, but it would cost the Messiah a bruised heel.

Apply this understanding by...

- identifying what kind of actions make a person a seed of the serpent or a seed of the woman (a Messiah-type person).
- evaluating your performance in those areas.
- celebrating where you are already succeeding.
- identifying positive changes you can make that will lead to further success.

women hate snakes (of course not *all* women hate snakes, but it is true as a general rule). Furthermore, God's words foreshadow the head-crushing women of the Old Testament (especially those in the book of Judges). Finally, God's words point forward to the Church, the bride of Christ, under whose feet God promises to crush Satan (Rom 16:20).

The mental picture
Of course, the serpent ultimately represents Satan, but resist the temptation to exchange the word serpent with Satan as you read Genesis 3. It's true, but not helpful at this point. There are two reasons for this. First, you are meant to see a mental picture as your read this passage—a serpent (dragon, sea beast, snake) getting his head crushed underfoot. This mental image will return many times throughout the Bible (for example, the crushing of Sisera's and Goliath's heads). Second, the serpent represents much more than Satan; it represents every person who identifies with Satan and follows in his footsteps—these are called the seed of the serpent in Genesis 3:15. Of course, when the Messiah comes another layer is added on; Christ died for even the enemies (serpent-people) of God, and redemption is offered to all mankind.

Likewise, the seed of the woman means Messiah, but don't mentally substitute the word Messiah here; it also means much more. The seed of the woman points to every righteous hero of the Bible who would defeat the enemies of God; Genesis 3:15 predicts in seed form (imagine that) much of what is to come in the Old Testament and New.

Finally, the promise of a seed to crush the head of the serpent points to the seed-*line*, a line of descendants that extends from Adam to Noah to Abraham to David to Christ. That seed-line is the thread of hope that runs all the way through the Old Testament.

Lesson 1.8

APPLICATION

Every relationship, every situation in life, every action brings with it the opportunity to act as a seed-person or a serpent-person. This lesson provides an opportunity to rethink who you are in your own story. Are you acting like a seed-person, confronting the enemy to bring deliverance to those who are being oppressed? Or are you acting like a serpent-person, afflicting others in wickedness? There is a stark contrast between these two types of people, and in most situations we find a mix of the two. But thinking through your life in stark terms like these gets the full range of options on the table. Identify a difficult situation in your life and determine how you are presently engaging in that situation. What can you do to move towards behaving like a seed-person? towards behaving like Jesus Christ?

ACTIVITIES

1. Imagination: Movies and Head Crushing. Many stories and movies retell the story of the Bible using different characters and actions. Think through some movies you've seen that have a head-crushing scene. (In *How to Train Your Dragon*, for example, the boy crushes the head of the bad dragon and loses his leg in the process.) Re-watch the scene if necessary, then answer the following questions. (Refer to Genesis 3:14-15.)

In the movie, which character is the "seed"? _____

In the movie, which character is the "serpent"? _____

In the movie, what does the seed do to the serpent? _____

In the movie, what does the serpent do to the seed? _____

What other similarities do you see between this movie and the biblical Story? _____

57

Unit 1: Creation and Fall

2. Draw It. Draw a picture of a hero crushing a serpent's head and the hero's heel getting bruised in the process. Be creative, but make sure you include the following in your drawing.

- The picture must have a serpent of some form.
- The serpent must be getting his head crushed in some way.
- There must be a person accomplishing the crushing.
- The person accomplishing the crushing must be receiving an injury in the process.

3. Celebration. In the space below, write a short prayer reflecting on Psalm 8 or 91. _____
_____
_____
_____
_____
_____

EVALUATION

1. Who is the seed of the serpent? _____
_____
_____
_____
_____
_____

2. Who is the seed of the woman? _____
_____
_____
_____
_____
_____

3. Who is the enemy in Genesis 3? _____
_____

4. What does head-crushing represent? _____
_____
_____

5. What does heel-bruising represent? _____
_____
_____

6. What is God telling you when you see a serpent crawling on his belly? _____
_____
_____
_____
_____

LESSON 1.9

Consequences: Pain in Childbearing, Toil, Expulsion from the Garden

THE STORY

Lesson Theme - Formal consequences of sin

After cursing the serpent, God turned his attention back to Adam and Eve. Even though the serpent was the enemy, Adam and Eve were guilty of sin, and there were consequences. Adam and Eve were created to be fruitful and multiply and to fill the earth and subdue. The purposes remained intact after the fall, but they were both made significantly harder.

God addressed Eve first. He told her that pain in childbirth would be greatly increased (multiplied). This meant that the "be fruitful and multiply" aspect of the creation mandate would now be significantly more difficult for the woman. God also said to the woman, "Your desire shall be for your husband, and he shall rule over you" (Gen 3:16b). This desire is not a reference to sexual desire, but, rather, a desire to pervert the creation order by exercising dominance over her husband. When the woman was tempted, she gave the fruit to Adam to eat, and he submitted to her. So from the fall forward, all women inherit this desire to exercise authority over their husbands from Eve. But the woman's desire to dominate would be frustrated, and her husband would respond with harsh lordship rather than godly leadership. Many of the difficulties in marriage are rooted in this aspect of the fall.

Adam's part of the creation mandate, subduing the earth, was also made much more difficult because the ground was cursed on account of him. It would now produce thorns and thistles and would require great toil and sweat to be productive. Additionally, the toil would seem vain since eventually man would become a part of the ground that he was working so hard to make productive: "for dust you are and to dust you shall return" (Gen 3:19b).

OVERVIEW

Having pronounced a curse upon the serpent and the hope of redemption for Adam and Eve, God now addressed the man and the woman and distributed the formal consequences for sin. Eve would have great pain in childbirth and a frustrated desire to rule over her husband. On account of Adam's sin, the earth was cursed and would only produce fruit with great toil; furthermore, Adam would return to dust at the end of his days. But, Adam understood the promise of a seed to crush the serpent's head, so in spite of knowing that everyone would face physical death, he named the woman Eve because she would be the mother of all the living. God offered the first sacrifice and made them coverings as well as kingly garments. He then sent them out to work the ground east of the garden, setting up guards on the east, so that they wouldn't eat from the tree of life without first going through death.

SOURCE MATERIAL

- Genesis 3:16-24
- Psalm 127
- Proverbs 3:33

Unit 1: Creation and Fall

OBJECTIVES

Feel...

- the tragic yet hopeful consequences of sin.
- gratitude for God's grace even as He dealt out consequences for sin.
- a sense of loss on account of broken relationships and banishment from the garden.

Understand...

- the formal consequences of sin for woman: painful child bearing and frustrated desire to rule over her husband.
- the formal consequences of sin for man: cursed earth and return to dust.
- that Adam named the woman "Eve," the mother of all the living, because he believed God's promise.
- the symbolism of the garments of skin God made: a picture of sacrifice and authority.
- that it was gracious for God to banish Adam and Eve from the garden and prevent them from eating from the tree of life without dying first.
- that Adam and Eve were sent out to the east of the garden, the side protected by cherubim.

Apply this understanding by...

- thanking God for graciously limiting the consequences for sin.
- thanking God that creation labor and family are still a blessing even if they are broken.
- considering areas of your life where you are trusting your own efforts to cover your sin rather than trusting in God's grace.

In Genesis 3:20 Adam gives his wife a name. "Adam named his wife Eve, because she would become the mother of all the living" (Gen 3:20, NIV). Notice that this verse follows directly after "for dust you are and to dust you shall return." What we would expect to hear is that Eve would become the mother of *all those who die*, but instead, we hear the exact opposite. By naming the woman Eve, Adam showed that he believed the promise of a seed (descendant) of the woman who would crush the head of the serpent. Not only that, but Adam also showed that he understood what this promise would mean for mankind. If the serpent's head was crushed, sin and death would be defeated; and restoration, redemption and even *resurrection* would be not only possible, but assured. Even though death would be a part of man's experience, Eve would be the mother of all the living. Adam's action indicates that he believed the promise of a coming Messiah.

In Genesis 3:21, God made "tunics of skin" for Adam and Eve. There are several layers of meaning here worth looking at. First, this was the first physical death in all of creation and the first substitution sacrifice. Instead of Adam dying, an animal died in his place. From this sacrifice, Adam and Eve were "covered." Certainly their physical bodies, but on a deeper level, their sin and shame were covered. (Note also that this implies that God rejected their own attempts to cover their sin and shame with fig leaves.) Additionally, the Hebrew word here for tunic means "coat-like robe," and throughout the Bible it is representative of authority. God clothed Adam and Eve as kings and queens; God was getting ready to send them out to rule over the earth. This was a blessing, but it was also tragic. Adam and Eve were like rebellious children, kicked out of the house prematurely. Their Father was sending them out to rule over creation, but they were not properly trained and prepared. They knew good and evil through rebellious behavior, not through wise training.

And so God banished Adam and Eve from the garden (Gen 3:23). They were sent out to the east of the garden to till the ground (we know they were sent to the east because the cherubim protected the garden on the east side—Gen 3:24). And again, though their banishment was tragic, it was also gracious. Now that sin was in the world, access to the tree of life could only come on the condition of death (ultimately, the death of the Messiah whose flesh and blood were given as food and drink which give life— John 6:53-54). To permit Adam and Eve to eat from the tree of life *before* death would mean glory without suffering—false glory; it would mean life without dealing with sin—false life. And to protect access to the tree of life, God put cherubim on the east side of the garden to guard the way. If Adam and Eve wanted back to the tree of life, they would have to pass through the angel's flaming sword, *death*.

APPLICATION

In Lesson 1.7, we looked at the natural consequences of sin, a reality that still exists in the world: you reap what you sow. In this lesson we looked at the formal consequence of the fall—the ones which God explicitly delineated and enforced. Likewise, there are still formal consequences in the world— enforced by God-ordained authorities in our lives such as parents, church and government. Think through a time when you sinned and experienced formal consequences enforced by an authority in your life (parents, especially). Which consequences are worse, formal or natural? Of course, just like natural consequences, formal consequences can leave you feeling ashamed; confess your sins and let the grace of God wash over you!

ACTIVITIES

1. Before and After. On the left side of the line below draw a picture of Adam and Eve before the fall, then on the right draw a picture of life after the fall. Below the drawings, list the differences between the two.

Lesson 1.9

2. Drawing: The Land of Eden after the Fall. Draw the following on the diagram below:

- Adam and Eve after the fall
- The cherubim guarding the entry on the east

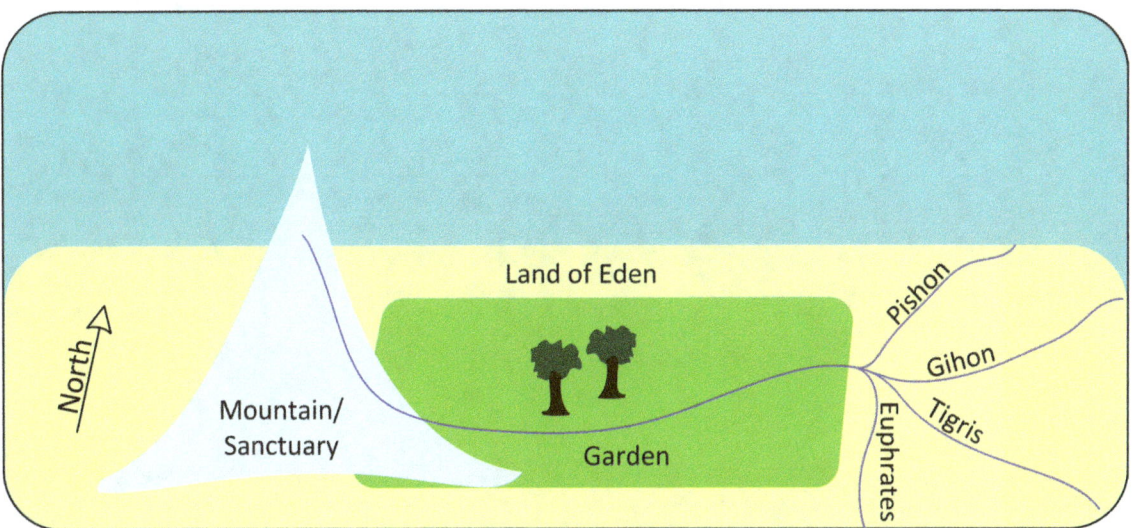

3. Read Psalm 127 and Proverbs 3:33 and write a prayer of praise and thanksgiving for the gift of family. _____
_____
_____
_____
_____
_____
_____
_____
_____
_____
_____
_____
_____

Unit 1: Creation and Fall

4. Imagination: Cherubim. Draw a picture of what the cherubim and the flaming sword might have looked like.

Lesson 1.9

EVALUATION

1. What were the formal consequences of sin for Eve? _____

2. What were the formal consequences for Adam? _____

3. Why did Adam name the woman "Eve"? _____

4. Why did God make Adam and Eve clothes of skin? _____

5. Why did God banish Adam and Eve from the garden? _____

6. What did God do to prevent Adam and Eve from going back to the garden? _____

UNIT 2: HUMANITY POISONED

Eve looked to her firstborn son, Cain, to fulfill the promise of Genesis 3:15, but he fell woefully short. Cain first failed in his priestly responsibilities in worship, then made it worse by murdering his brother rather than repenting. The murder cost Cain his livelihood, but he remained unrepentant even though God showed him mercy. Cain's sin grew even greater in his descendants, and the failure was in high relief by the time we get down the line to Lamech who turned God's mercy upon Cain into a personal boast. To replace Abel, God gave Adam and Eve a son named Seth, whose descendants would carry on the chosen seed-line. His line reestablished Yahweh worship, and his descendants walked with God. There was even a good Lamech in Seth's line who foretold that his son Noah would bring comfort to God's people.

Adam and Cain's sin had spread so badly that the whole earth was filled with violence. God regretted making man and decided to destroy all of humanity and start over with Noah and his family. God commanded Noah to build an ark according to His specifications and to bring on it his family, animals and enough food to survive the flood. God then undid the third day of creation, covering all the dry land with water again.

When the rains ceased and the waters receded, Noah, his family and the animals went out of the ark into a new world. The first thing Noah did in the re-created world was to act as a priest and offer an ascension offering. In response, God decided to never again destroy every living thing with a flood. God blessed and commissioned Noah as He had Adam, but with greater (kingly) responsibility. Man now had the power of life and death: the ability to eat meat and the responsibility to carry out capital punishment. God promised never again to judge the earth with a flood; it was now man's responsibility to prevent the earth from being filled with violence. God sealed His covenant with the sign of the rainbow, a picture of God's peace and blessing upon the earth.

Rather than scattering to fulfill God's commission to take dominion over the earth, some of Noah's descendants rebelled, gathering in the plains of Shinar. By building a great city and tower, they hoped to make a name for themselves and not be scattered throughout the earth. Knowing that they would succeed if left unchecked, God confused their languages and scattered them anyway, preventing their project from succeeding.

LESSON 2.1

UNIT 2

Eve's Hope Delayed—The First Seed Murdered by a Serpent: Cain and Abel

THE STORY

Lesson Theme - The hope that Cain or Abel would be the promised seed was crushed.

In Genesis 3:15 God promised that a descendant of the woman, a son of Eve, would crush the head of the serpent and therefore redeem mankind and all of creation. It is almost certain that Adam, and perhaps especially Eve, believed this promise. Eve's words in Genesis 4:1, "I have acquired a man from the LORD," indicate that she thought Cain would be the promised deliverer. This same yearning that Eve had for the fulfillment of the promise is a hope that continues throughout the Old Testament to create a desire that Christ would ultimately fulfill.

In Genesis 4:1, Adam and Eve conceived and had their first son. Notice the continuance of the creation pattern (command into existence, divide, name, evaluate) in the second generation. Like a theme in music, the pattern isn't repeated slavishly, but it is recognizably present. In verses 1-2, Adam and Eve created and named their first two sons. Then in the following verses, God tested (divided) and judged (evaluated) their actions.

Cain and Abel had both apparently learned from their parents the necessity to worship God and offer sacrifices to Him. Abel was a shepherd, while Cain worked the ground, so when they brought offerings, they each brought something from the fruits of their labor; Cain brought some crops he had harvested, while Abel brought an animal from his flocks (Gen 4:3-4). God accepted Abel's offering, but not Cain's.

OVERVIEW

Eve looked to her firstborn son, Cain, to fulfill the promise of Genesis 3:15, but he fell woefully short. Cain first failed in his responsibilities in worship; and then, when God gave him the opportunity to repent and correct himself, he murdered Abel instead. As a consequence, Cain lost his whole livelihood, but remained unrepentant to the end. But God showed Cain mercy in the midst of His judgment.

SOURCE MATERIAL

- Genesis 4:1-15
- Psalms 32, 51
- Proverbs 29:1

Most people reading this passage want to know why Abel's offering was accepted and Cain's was not. A few answers are possible. This is a case where we need to pay attention to what we know for sure and what is just speculation. We may speculate that God required blood sacrifice, which Abel fulfilled, but Cain did not. However, throughout the Old Testament, vegetable offerings were also required, so it's not certain that was the problem. The text mentions that Abel's offering was from the firstlings of his flock, while it makes no parallel assertion about Cain's offerings being the firstfruits of his garden. It is possible that the offering was supposed to be a firstfruits offering, and Cain failed to bring the first and best produce. We don't know for sure. What we do know for sure is this: Cain's heart

Unit 2: Humanity Poisoned

OBJECTIVES

Feel...

- shock at Cain's choice to kill Abel rather than just repent.
- awareness of your own tendency to deny sin and attack people who are doing better.

Understand...

- that even though we don't know exactly what Cain did wrong when he offered his sacrifice, we do know that he did something wrong and that he knew it.
- that Cain could have easily solved the problems created by his sin by simply asking God what he needed to do to make it right and then doing it.
- that God was merciful to Cain; He gave him many chances to repent and was even merciful in Cain's punishment.
- that God is present in our lives, and we have to face Him constantly, even when we do wrong.
- that God seeks to correct us, not just to punish us.
- that there are consequences to our actions, and the consequences are magnified if we don't repent.
- that even in judgment on unrepentant sin, God shows mercy.

Apply this understanding by...

- considering how you want to deny your own sin rather than repent and own up to it.
- considering what it cost Cain to refuse to repent, and how that same dynamic might play out in your own life.

was not right, and Abel's was; and whatever it was that Cain did wrong, *he* knew it, because the way God rebuked him showed that he knew what he ought to have done. The point is not exactly what Cain did wrong, but that he knew what he did wrong, and he was angry that he didn't get away with it.

God did not accept Cain's offering; this was a simple problem with a simple solution All Cain had to do was say, "Okay, God what do I need to do to make this right?" God would have told him and he could have made it right, right then and there.

Instead, Cain became sullen and angry (Gen 4:5). But even so, God, in His mercy, didn't immediately punish Cain; He approached him and asked him to do right (Gen 4:7). Rather than go back and offer the right sacrifice, Cain murdered his brother (Gen 4:8). While the story of Adam and Eve is about obeying God (or not), the story of Cain and Abel is about how we ought to respond when God calls out our disobedience.

Even after Cain had murdered his brother, God did not immediately punish him, but approached him once again. "Where is Abel your brother?" God asked Cain, presenting him with another chance to come clean and make things right; but, again, Cain didn't take this opportunity for mercy (Gen 4:9).

Finally, God did punish Cain by taking away the thing that was most important to him: his ability to work the ground to produce a crop. Cain was a worker of the ground (Gen 4:2) and brought an offering from the fruit of the ground to the Lord (Gen 4:3). He killed Abel in the field, then Abel's blood cried out from the ground (Gen 4:10), and so Cain was cursed from the ground, meaning that the ground would no longer be fruitful for him as it once was (Gen 4:11-12a).

In addition to making the ground unfruitful for Cain, God declared that he would be a fugitive and vagabond (Gen 4:12b). Cain (perhaps being a bit dramatic after all that he had done against God) complained that his punishment was too heavy; he was concerned that someone would find him and kill him (people tend to fear that others are wicked in the same ways they are) (Gen 4:14).

But even in judgment, God heard Cain's concerns and responded to them. God marked Cain as an indication of His promise to avenge sevenfold anyone who killed him (Gen 4:15). However, as we will see with Lamech (Gen 4:23-24), Cain's family turned God's promise from an expression of mercy to a reason for boasting.

APPLICATION

Cain is a negative example for us, and the tendency with negative examples is to make them irrelevant by saying, "But I'm not like that." However, we are all like Cain; surely you can recognize in your own heart the same tendency to justify yourself and deny God's conviction. Contemplating Cain's story teaches us the value of repentance. Cain's denials and anger just drove him deeper into sin; but as hard as it often sounds to our prideful hearts, repentance is actually pretty simple and, in a very short amount of time, solves all the problems our sin has created.

ACTIVITIES

1. Cain's Loss. Highlight all the words in Genesis 4:1-15 (NIV below) related to the ground: soil, ground, land, field, etc. Then answer the questions below.

> [1]Adam made love to his wife Eve, and she became pregnant and gave birth to Cain. She said, "With the help of the Lord I have brought forth a man." [2]Later she gave birth to his brother Abel.
>
> Now Abel kept flocks, and Cain worked the soil. [3]In the course of time Cain brought some of the fruits of the soil as an offering to the Lord. [4]And Abel also brought an offering—fat portions from some of the firstborn of his flock. The Lord looked with favor on Abel and his offering, [5]but on Cain and his offering he did not look with favor. So Cain was very angry, and his face was downcast.
>
> [6]Then the Lord said to Cain, "Why are you angry? Why is your face downcast? [7]If you do what is right, will you not be accepted? But if you do not do what is right, sin is crouching at your door; it desires to have you, but you must rule over it."
>
> [8]Now Cain said to his brother Abel, "Let's go out to the field." While they were in the field, Cain attacked his brother Abel and killed him.

Unit 2: Humanity Poisoned

⁹Then the Lord said to Cain, "Where is your brother Abel?"

"I don't know," he replied. "Am I my brother's keeper?"

¹⁰The Lord said, "What have you done? Listen! Your brother's blood cries out to me from the ground. ¹¹Now you are under a curse and driven from the ground, which opened its mouth to receive your brother's blood from your hand. ¹²When you work the ground, it will no longer yield its crops for you. You will be a restless wanderer on the earth."

¹³Cain said to the Lord, "My punishment is more than I can bear. ¹⁴Today you are driving me from the land, and I will be hidden from your presence; I will be a restless wanderer on the earth, and whoever finds me will kill me."

¹⁵But the Lord said to him, "Not so; anyone who kills Cain will suffer vengeance seven times over." Then the Lord put a mark on Cain so that no one who found him would kill him.

What is Cain's relationship to the ground at the beginning of the story? _____
_____
_____

How does Cain's relationship with the ground change over the course of the story? _____
_____
_____

What lessons can you draw out of Cain's changed relationship with the ground? _____
_____
_____

2. Cain choosing to kill Abel seems surprising to us. What do you think might have been going on inside Cain's heart to make killing Abel seem like a reasonable idea? It might help to reflect on the kind of reasoning you have done leading up to committing a sin. _____
_____
_____
_____
_____
_____

Lesson 2.1

3. Journal Time. Read through Psalm 32 or 51 as well as Proverbs 29:1, then spend some time answering the questions below.

Has God ever taken something away from you because of a sin you committed? _____
_____
_____

Did God give you a chance to repent of the sin? _____
_____
_____

How could you have handled the situation differently? _____
_____
_____

EVALUATION

1. What does Eve's statement in Genesis 4:1 indicate about her understanding of Genesis 3:15? _____
_____

2. What are some speculations we can make as to why God did not accept Cain's sacrifice? What do we know for sure about God's disapproval of Cain's offering? _____
_____
_____
_____

3. God did not respect Cain's offering. How did God respond to Cain? _____
_____

4. What would have happened if Cain had listened to God's challenge in Genesis 4:7? _____
_____

5. How did God show mercy to Cain through this story? _____
_____
_____
_____

The Descendants of Cain and Seth

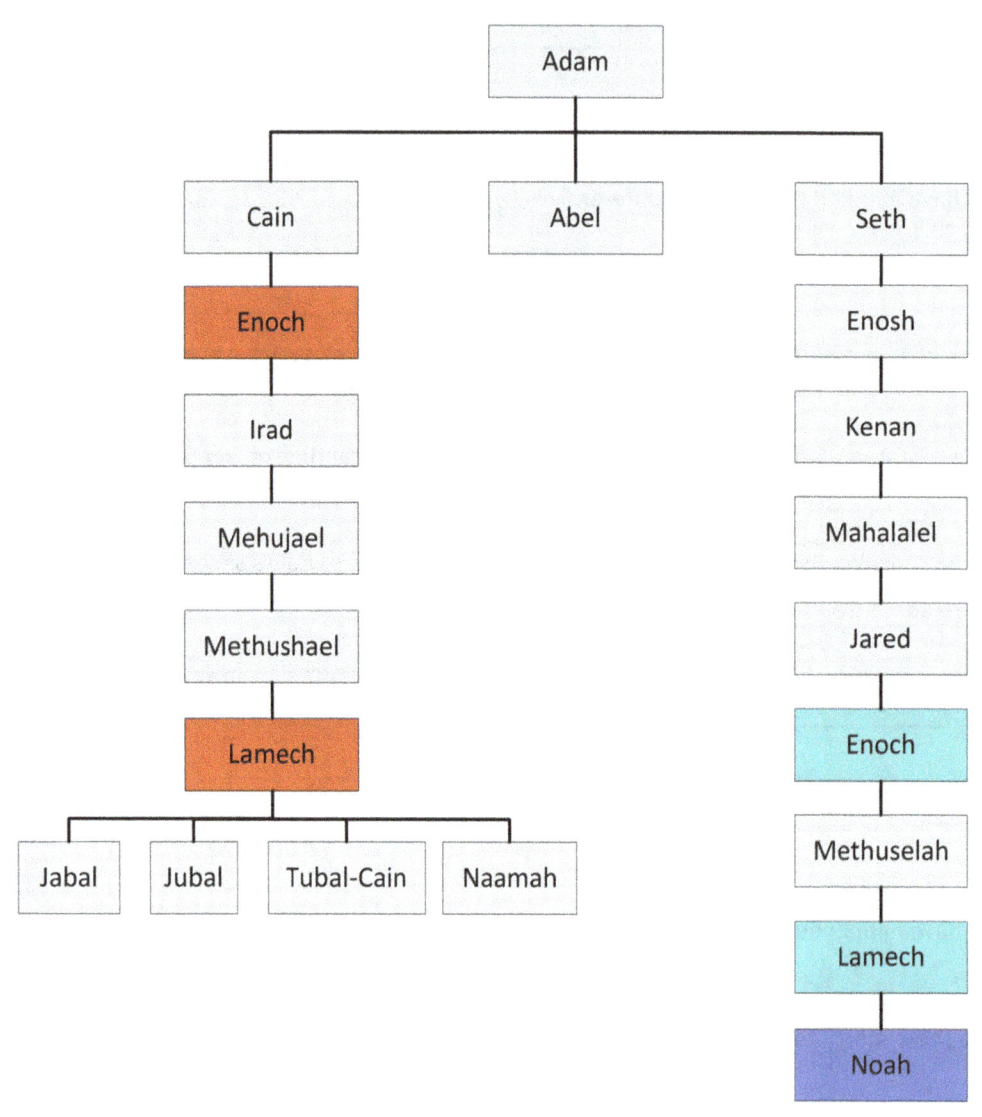

LESSON 2.2

Cain's Wicked Line and a New Seed-Line Chosen

UNIT 2

THE STORY

Lesson Theme - Cain's line rejected and a new seed line chosen

Adam and Eve hoped that Cain would be the promised seed-son, but he turned out to be a murderer. As a result, his entire line was poisoned—destined to great power and great wickedness. Seth's line contrasts nicely with Cain's. Where Cain's line failed, Seth's line, while certainly not perfect, showed a much higher level of faithfulness toward God.

Cain's line

After God had settled Cain's punishment for murdering his brother, Cain went out of the land, had a son, and built a city (Gen 4:16-17). The hope of a glorious city was present even in the garden before Adam and Eve had sinned—they were made to take dominion over the world, which included building a city for God to dwell in. Before Cain murdered his brother, he was a man of the field; but now, having lost his ability to produce a crop from the ground, he set his hands to the task of city building.

When Adam and Eve were cast out of the garden, they were forced to begin the task of taking dominion of the earth before they were ready. Likewise, when God punished Cain, He forced him to begin the task of civilization before he was mature enough.

Of course, Cain's lack of maturity didn't mean that he and his line were not capable of building culture and civilization. They actually developed technology very rapidly; apparently sin does not

OVERVIEW

Cain's sin was magnified in his descendants, and ultimately, his line was rejected because of their failure. This failure was in high relief by the time we get down the line to Lamech who turned God's mercy upon Cain into a personal boast. To replace Abel, God gave Adam and Eve a son named Seth, whose descendants would carry on the chosen seed-line. His line reestablished Yahweh worship, and his descendants walked with God. There was even a good Lamech in Seth's line who foretold that his son Noah would bring comfort to God's people.

SOURCE MATERIAL

- Genesis 4:16-5:32
- Psalm 1
- Proverbs 3:30

necessarily prevent innovation and invention. After Cain had built the city of Enoch, his descendants developed a rich repertoire of cultural skills: animal husbandry (Gen 4:20), musical skill (Gen 4:21), and iron and bronze craftsmanship (Gen 4:22).

The problem was the purpose of the civilization that Cain and his line had built. Cain named the city that he built after his son, Enoch; he was aiming to build his line, his name into an enduring city. Nothing is said in Genesis 4:16-17 about God or His glory. Cain had rejected his Creator

Unit 2: Humanity Poisoned

OBJECTIVES

Feel...

- a sense of victory that God chose Seth to replace Abel so we would not be stuck with Cain's line.
- disgust at the bad Lamech's twisted view of God's mercy upon Cain.
- awe at the righteousness displayed in Seth's line.

Understand...

- how Cain's sins got more exaggerated as they were passed through the generations.
- how Cain's line failed as a result of their sin and Seth's line replaced them as the seed-line.
- the differences between Cain's line and Seth's line.
- that God choosing Seth's line was a fulfillment of His promise that a seed of the woman would crush the head of the serpent.

Apply this understanding by...

- evaluating your life to see if you are using your gifts and talents for the Lord's glory.
- recognizing, that as believers in Jesus, we are in Seth's line.
- asking yourself whether you act more like a descendant of Cain or of Seth.
- asking yourself what changes you could make in your life to be more suited to Seth's line.

quite forcefully and was now attempting to build what theologians have called the city of man.

Cain's own sinful tendencies were exaggerated in his descendants. Lamech was Cain's sin, gone to seed (Gen 4:23-24). God had promised to avenge Cain as an act of mercy, to prevent anyone from killing him; Lamech turned God's mercy into a boast and took his own vengeance in a sick parody of what God had promised: he killed a young man for hurting him. Cain's line was on a clear trajectory: increased power and accomplishment and increased wickedness—a nasty combination.

Seth's line

But God was not finished. He had promised that a descendant of the woman would crush the head of the serpent, and He was going to make good on His promise. Genesis 4:25-26 demonstrates that Eve understood God's promise. She had initially expected that Cain or Abel, perhaps, would be the promised son, but now it was clear that neither of them were the one.

"And Adam knew his wife again, and she bore a son and named him Seth, 'For God has appointed another seed for me instead of Abel, whom Cain killed.' And as for Seth, to him also a son was born; and he named him Enosh. Then men began to call on the name of the LORD" (Gen 4:25-26).

Eve hoped that this son, Seth, would be the one, the bearer of the seed-line through whom the head-crusher would ultimately come. And she was right.

Genesis 5 begins with a condensed repeat of the creation narrative. Adam was created in the image and likeness of God, and Seth was born to Adam in *his* image and likeness. Here was a son who was like his Father in heaven. The hope of redemption is again reinforced.

In the genealogy recorded in the remainder of Genesis 5, several contrasts are set up between wicked Cain's line and righteous Seth's line. There was a good Enoch (Seth's line) as well as a bad one (Cain's line); there was also a good Lamech and a bad one.

Cain named his son Enoch, and then named his city Enoch as well—an earthly legacy for his son. In contrast, the Sethite Enoch walked with God, and God took him up to heaven (Gen 5:24). The seed-line came through the Enoch in heaven, not the Enoch on earth.

The words of both Lamechs are recorded in Genesis, and both spoke not only of the past, but also of the future. But while the Cainite Lamech promised murder and violence, the Sethite Lamech promised comfort and rest ("Noah" literally means "rest") (Gen 5:29). The Cainite Lamech also departed from original marriage customs by taking a second wife (Gen 4:23).

In the midst of this record of Seth's line, however, nothing is said about them building civilization and culture. They may have, but they were, at the very least, behind the technological curve. Regardless, it was not yet time for God to build His city, and the earth was, by this time, overflowing with the wickedness of Cain's line (Gen 6:5).

APPLICATION

Cain was clearly very intelligent and capable. He built a city before there were cities, and his descendants developed technology very rapidly. In themselves, there is nothing wrong with civilization and technology, but apart from God, Cain's developing civilization only served to spread wickedness throughout the world quite efficiently.

We are all born with talents—special gifting from God. But with these gifts comes the sobering reality that we can indeed use them for our own vainglory, which in turn only serves to further our own wickedness. What gifts and abilities has God given you? Are you using them for your glory or for the Lord's?

Seth and Cain's lines also provide us with a sharp contrast of how to live; Psalm 1 encourages us to avoid the path of the wicked and walk in the way of the righteous—avoid the path of Cain and walk in the way of Seth. We can take a positive lesson from the Sethite Lamech: be a source of comfort and hope for the people of God. From the Cainite Lamech, we can take a negative lesson: don't fight for the sake of pride or sheer violence: "Don't strive with a man without cause..." (Prov 3:30).

ACTIVITIES

1. The Seed-Line. God promised in Genesis 3:15 that a seed of the woman would crush the head of the serpent. We can track this promise by following a line of descendants that leads to the promised Son. Find a large piece of paper, then work vertically down the page starting with Adam at the top, then the chosen seed-line son of Adam just below that and then working your way down to Noah following the line given in Genesis 5. Keep this paper, you'll be adding to it in the future.

2. Reading aloud. Read Genesis 5 out loud emphasizing the repeated phrase "and he died." Reflect below on the effect of the repeated phrase. What did you learn? _____
_____
_____
_____

3. Compare and Contrast: Cain's Line and Seth's Line. Make a list of all of the contrasts between Cain's line and Seth's line below.

Cain	Seth

4. Journal Time: Living in Seth's Line. Read Psalm 1, then spend some time considering the following questions.

If you are a believer in Jesus, you are in Seth's line. Do you live like you are a member of Seth's seed-line? Why or why not? _____
_____
_____
_____

What could you change about your life to better reflect the fact that you are in Seth's line? _____
_____
_____
_____

Lesson 2.2

EVALUATION

1. Why did Cain's line fail as the seed-line? _____

2. Whose line did God choose to be the new seed-line? _____

3. How was Lamech's sin similar to Cain's? How was it different than Cain's? _____

4. Compare and contrast the two Enochs and the two Lamechs. _____

5. Why does Genesis 5 begin by reiterating that God made Adam and Eve in His likeness? _____

6. Why was it important for the author to name three of Noah's sons in Genesis 5:32, instead of just one, like everyone else in the line? _____

LESSON 2.3

The Flood

UNIT 2

THE STORY

Lesson Theme - God replaced Adam with Noah. God rejected Adam as the head of humanity, choosing a new seed in his place. The flood was a death and resurrection; Adam (mankind) was dying and being resurrected *in* the chosen seed Noah. The earth was also going through a death and resurrection; it would be baptized in the waters of the flood (baptism by immersion is a picture of death throughout the Bible). Noah is a picture of the Messiah: he was a preacher of righteousness (2 Pet 2:5); he was perfectly faithful to God (notice how many times the text says that Noah obeyed everything the Lord commanded him to do); he was a savior of the remnant of humanity who passed through the flood.

The fall of Adam and Eve was the first fall of mankind. The flood was the second fall. The whole race had failed to be what God called it to be, and so the race would surely die. God took out one family from which to begin a new world. As the story unfolds, we will hear about the tower of Babel, which was the third fall of mankind. God would ultimately call Abram in order to resolve all three of these falls.

Genesis 6:1-4 explains the level of wickedness that had developed on the earth. Apparently, fallen angels ("sons of God" is used as a reference to angels in the Old Testament; see Job 1:6) were marrying the daughters of men and having children by them. It is the fathers of these "daughters of men" who are being implicitly indicted here. They should have been protecting

OVERVIEW

Adam and Cain's sin had spread to the entire earth, and wickedness was abounding everywhere. Noah, however, found favor in God's eyes. God regretted making man and decided to destroy all of humanity and start over with Noah and his family. So God commanded Noah to build an ark according to His specifications and to bring on it his family, animals and enough food to survive the flood. God then destroyed the earth and everything in it with a flood.

SOURCE MATERIAL

- Genesis 6-7
- Psalm 29
- Proverbs 2:22

their daughters, but, instead, were giving them away freely.

Setting aside the complexities of what this might mean, let's just say that man's wickedness abounded so much that some very strange things were happening on the earth at this time. We do know for sure that it was *not* the strange actions of angels or the existence of evil giants that led to God's judgement on earth but the evil deeds of the offspring of Adam.

It's easy to despair of the wickedness of our society, but we can be certain that we are not nearly as wicked as the society in the period of

Unit 2: Humanity Poisoned

OBJECTIVES

Feel...

- disgusted by the wickedness of the earth before the flood.
- thankful for Noah's faithfulness in spite of the wickedness around him.
- awe at God's power and wrath in the flood.

Understand...

- that the flood was the second fall of mankind and constituted God's rejection of Adam as the head of humanity.
- that Noah was a temporary replacement of Adam and a picture of Christ; ultimately Christ would be the head.
- that the flood was a death and resurrection of (1) humanity and (2) the earth.
- that in order to be faithful to His promise of a seed to crush the head of the serpent, God had to preserve a seed through the flood, and Noah was that seed.
- that Noah obeyed everything God commanded him to do, even though he was surrounded by wickedness.
- what was on the ark: Noah, his wife, his three sons and their three wives, two of each animal and seven of each clean animal (for sacrificing).

Apply this understanding by...

- evaluating your life in relation to Noah's and considering how you should act when you are surrounded by wickedness.
- worshiping the Lord because of the power, glory and wrath of God as revealed in the flood.

time before the flood. We have a judicial system that has it's roots in God's word; the Church still has moderate influence in our culture. Not so during Noah's time: "every intent of the thoughts of [man's] heart was only evil continually" (Gen 6:5), and there was nothing to restrain man's wicked intents. The earth was *full* of violence.

In contrast to all of the other descendants of Adam, Seth's line through Enoch and Lamech, leading to Noah, walked with God. By the time Noah was an adult, everyone else had departed from God, but Noah found favor in the eyes of the Lord (Gen 6:8).

Notice God's reaction to man's wickedness: He was grieved that He had made man (literally "Adam" in Hebrew) (Gen 6:6). God made Adam; Adam disobeyed his father and betrayed his wife. Adam passed his wickedness on to his son Cain, who took his father's wickedness to the next level and killed his brother. Cain passed his wickedness on to his entire line. Now, the sinfulness of Adam had spread to the entire world; betrayal, murder, father-hatred and all sorts of wickedness were a part of the life of every man. God experienced this wickedness with deep sadness and regretted that He had ever made Adam.

The story of Noah as familiar: God took counsel with Noah and told him His plan to destroy the earth, then commanded Noah to build the ark and told him how to build it. After that, God told Noah to bring on the ark two of every creature, seven of each clean sacrificial animal, his family, as well as food for all. And finally, God brought a worldwide flood upon the earth.

The flood is a compelling picture of God's glory as displayed in His wrath and powerful judgment. This judgment on the earth was completely in line with God's character. We're shocked by the

sudden and dramatic nature of the judgement, but Proverbs says that the wicked are wiped off the face of the earth (Prov 2:22). *That's just what happens in God's world*. However, don't fall into the temptation to set God's wrath against his love. Wrath is the expression of offended love; love that goes unreturned. Before God brings the flood on the earth, he is grieved at mankind and expresses sorrow over creation (Gen 6:7). His wrath comes out of the pain over the mess man has made of his good and perfect gifts.

Noah, chosen by God as the patriarch of the family that would repopulate the earth is also the chosen bearer of the seed-line. The earth has undergone a death and resurrection, a baptism under the waters of the flood. Now after the flood, Noah is a new Adam, and a new seed-son; God couldn't just wipe out the whole earth and start over, he had to keep his promise that a descendant of Eve would save the world. Noah is realization of faithfulness of God post-flood.

APPLICATION

Noah showed incredible faithfulness to God in the midst of a world absolutely full of wickedness. He was almost certainly mocked for worshiping Yahweh and building a big boat. It is so tempting to morph and conform to whatever wickedness happens to be around us; even in just small ways. Noah's example is a model of resisting peer pressure and being faithful to God even when it costs a lot.

ACTIVITIES

1. Imagination. To get your mind around what the world might have been like before the flood, imagine what the world would be like today if there were no major restraining influences: no churches, no code of laws based on the Bible, no Christians. Write a 3-5 paragraphs on a separate sheet of paper describing what a normal day would be like for you in such a society.

2. Video. Read through Psalm 29, then search online for a video from a tsunami. Take in the devastation and imagine how much worse the flood would have been. Write down some of you reactions in the space below.

How did you picture the biblical flood before viewing the video? _____

_____
_____
_____
_____
_____

Unit 2: Humanity Poisoned

How do you picture the biblical flood now? _____
_____
_____
_____

How does this affect your view of God? _____
_____
_____
_____

3. Reflection. Answer the following questions.

Why do you think Noah was able to be faithful to God even when there was so much pressure to live an evil life? _____
_____
_____
_____
_____
_____

How can we act more like Noah in order to be faithful to God even when we may be surrounded by wickedness? _____
_____
_____
_____
_____
_____
_____

Lesson 2.3

EVALUATION

1. What was the first fall of mankind? The flood was what fall of mankind? _____

2. Why did God choose Noah? _____

3. What does the flood picture? _____

4. What was the main difference between Adam and Noah? _____

5. How did Noah act when he was surrounded by the wickedness of the world? _____

LESSON 2.4

God's Covenant with Noah and the New Creation

THE STORY

Lesson Theme - Noah was the new Adam of the new creation.

After the flood, God made Noah into the new Adam, the head over the new creation. Humanity had died in Adam and was resurrected in Noah. You will notice similarities and differences in God's commissions to Adam and Noah. One big difference is that God established a covenant with Noah; God never did this with Adam. The commission and covenant that God made with Noah is still in effect; we are reminded of this every time we see the rainbow.

The ark at rest

After 150 days, God remembered Noah in the ark (Gen 8:1). Notice how the command and divide aspects of God's creative pattern are repeated in the beginning of Genesis 8 as He brought forth His new creation. God caused the flood to recede (command). A wind passed over the face of the earth while the water receded, much like in Genesis 1:2 when the Spirit (same word for breath or wind) hovered over the face of the waters before God. Over time, the water level continued to drop until dry ground appeared—God separated land from water (divide). This was a new creation, and Noah was the new Adam.

In Genesis 8:6-14, Noah sent birds out of the ark while the water receded. The birds provide a symbolic picture of death and resurrection in the new creation. Noah first sent out a raven. As a scavenger, the raven presumably fed off the carrion of the old creation (this is why the raven kept going back and forth until the waters dried up—Gen 8:7). Noah then sent out a dove, but

OVERVIEW

The rains ceased and the water began to recede. Noah sent out a raven as the old creation died and then a dove as the new creation came to life. Noah and his family and the animals then left the ark. The first act of obedience Noah performed in the new creation was to offer an ascension offering, which pleased God. God then blessed and commissioned Noah like He had Adam, only now He allowed people to eat meat and gave a provision for capital punishment. Finally, God made a covenant with Noah and the creation that He would never again bring a flood to destroy the earth. God sealed His covenant with the sign of the rainbow, a picture of God's peace and blessing upon the earth.

SOURCE MATERIAL

- Genesis 8:1-9:17
- Psalm 66
- Proverbs 25:28

while the old creation was finishing the process of death, the dove would not stay out. After seven days, however, Noah once again sent out the dove, and it found an olive leaf, a sign of life. After another seven days, the dove did not return since the old creation had died off and the new creation was fully alive (Gen 8:12).

Noah's offering

When the waters had finally completely dried up, Noah and his family and all the animals got

Unit 2: Humanity Poisoned

OBJECTIVES

Feel...

- joy and hope in the new creation that Noah was now the head of.
- excited about the peaceful beginning to the new creation in contrast to the fall of the first creation.

Understand...

- that Noah (the seed) was now the new Adam, the new head over the new creation.
- that the new creation was the old creation in baptized and resurrected form.
- that the raven represents the dying old creation, and the dove represents new life.
- that the ascension offering Noah gave was an act of consecration.
- that God blessed and commissioned Noah in a similar way as He did Adam.
- what a covenant is: a contract that establishes a relationship and what the nature of the covenant was between God and Noah.
- that the rainbow is a symbol of peace.
- the nature of the curse on Canaan: he would be a servant of Shem.

Apply this understanding by...

- recognizing that Noah was a picture of Christ and was called to rule over a new creation.
- giving thanks and offering your life to God as Noah did.
- evaluating your response to difficulty over the past week.

off the ark. Noah's first act of obedience in the new creation was to offer a sacrifice. This was, in fact, the very reason that he brought seven of every clean animal onto the ark. Notice that Noah offered a sacrifice from *every* clean animal he had with him, which was likely a huge number of offerings. These offerings are called *burnt* offerings (Gen 8:20) and is the first time this designation comes up in the Bible, though we will see it many more times. The Hebrew word that is translated as "burnt" in most English translations actually means "ascension," and so these sacrifices are more properly called ascension offerings. When the animal was burned on the altar, the smoke would ascend to the presence of the Lord. The smoke represented the worshiper consecrating himself to God. Noah was consecrating himself and his family to God and was, in effect, saying, "You are our God, we are Your people, and this is Your creation." Unlike Adam and Cain, Noah was a good priest and began the resurrected creation with a priestly offering to God. Psalm 66 reflects on the proper response to God's deliverance, which is very much the way Noah responded.

God's first response to Noah's offerings was pleasure because of the soothing aroma, the "smell" of His people offering themselves to Him (Gen 8:21a). Then God promised never again to curse the ground on account of man (Gen 3:21b). Although God did not revoke the curse on the ground He had given to Adam, the new creation started out with a promise of stability (Gen 8:22). Even though the ground was cursed, it would not get any worse; and though toil would be difficult, the harvest would not be revoked.

Noah blessed and commissioned
In Genesis 1, God blessed Adam and told him to fill the earth and subdue it. Noah was the new Adam in this new creation, and in Genesis 9, God gave Noah a similar blessing:

Lesson 2.4

- to be fruitful and multiply and fill the earth
- that the land animals, fish and birds would fear man and were given into man's hand
- that the animals were given as food for man
- that the green herbs were given as food

Then God gave two prohibitions:

- that man must not eat animals with blood in them
- that man must not kill another man; if he did, his life would be demanded

These prohibitions established civil government *for the purpose of enforcing justice* through the institution of capital punishment. It was now good and right for civil governments to create criminal laws and have means for enforcing those laws through courts of justice. This aspect of Noah's commission was the foundation upon which Israel's civil government was later built.

God then made *His* covenant with Noah (Gen 9:8-17). What is a covenant? In simple terms, a covenant is a contract that establishes the terms of a relationship between two parties. Marriage is the most common relational covenant and provides a good example: both the husband and the wife promise certain things that define their relationship. The husband will love the wife, the wife will submit to and obey the husband, and they promise sexual fidelity to each other. They then exchange rings (a tangible guarantee) as a sign of the covenant.

In the Noahic covenant, the parties to the covenant were (1) God and (2) Noah and his descendants and all the animals. God promised to never again destroy the earth with a flood. He then gave a sign of the covenant: He set His bow in the sky. The word for bow here is the same as the word for the weapon that shoots arrows. In essence, God was saying, "I have sent my wrath against man; I have made war on the earth; I now hang my bow on the wall." Thus, the bow is a symbol of peace between God and man.

Noah then planted a vineyard and made some wine (Gen 9:20). This was a good and right thing to do, especially in the new creation. When we come into the new creation, God's kingdom, we too will drink wine with the Lord. However, here Noah drank too much and fell asleep naked. Shamefully, Noah's son Ham observed the nakedness of his father (Gen 9:22). Because of Ham's misconduct, Canaan (Ham's son) was cursed, and it was prophesied that he would be Shem's servant (Gen 9:25-26). Shem would be next in the seed-line after Noah and would become the father of Abraham and the Jewish nation. Canaan, of course, fathered the Canaanites who would later be Israel's enemies. Noah's curse upon Canaan and blessing upon Shem set the precedent for the conquest of the land of Canaan and helps explain why the Israelites were commanded by God to treat the Canaanites the way they did.

APPLICATION

Noah was an image of Christ—God gave him a new creation to rule over like He gave Christ a new creation to rule over. A call to thanksgiving accompanies this stewardship. We have each been given a call to rule in our own lives, and this call should elicit thanksgiving and consecration. Our first duty is to rule over our own spirit, for our spirit is our first domain of authority from which all God-given rule flows (Prov 25:28).

Unit 2: Humanity Poisoned

ACTIVITIES

1. Discovery: God's Covenants. Read God's commissions to Adam and Noah in Genesis 1:28-30 and Genesis 9:1-7 and answer the questions below.

List the differences and similarities between the two commissions. _____

_____

_____

_____

We are governed today by God's commission to Noah. What does this mean for us in contrast to the world of Adam? _____

_____

_____

_____

2. Discovery: Re-creation. Genesis 8 is a re-creation of the earth and therefore contains a number of similarities to Genesis 1. Look in Genesis 8 to find as many similar events to Genesis 1 as you can. For example, dry ground appeared as the water receded just as the land was separated from the waters in Genesis 1. Use your imagination and creativity to see the similarities; it does not have to be a perfect analogy to count as a right answer. _____

Lesson 2.4

EVALUATION

1. How was Noah's response to the new creation different from Adam's response to creation? _____

2. What do the raven and the dove represent? _____

3. What is an ascension offering? _____

4. Name a difference between God's commission to Adam and His commission to Noah. _____

5. What is a covenant? _____

6. What did God promise in His covenant to Noah? _____

7. What does the rainbow mean? _____

8. Explain how the rainbow tells us of God's faithfulness. _____

9. What is the curse on Canaan? _____

LESSON 2.5

The Babylon Project—A Godless City Destroyed: The Tower of Babel

THE STORY

Lesson Theme - The city of man
Cain had built a city apart from any interest in bringing glory to God—the downstream result was a toxic and murderous civilization which ultimately led to the flood. You would think Noah's descendants would've learned from Cain's sin; but instead, shortly after the flood they went and did it again. Rejecting God's call to take dominion over the earth, at least some of Noah's descendants built a city called Babel, another city of man.

Background
Genesis 10 is known as the Table of Nations. It records the descendants of the three sons of Noah. There's a lot of information here, but there are just a few things we want to highlight in this lesson.

First, the descendants of Ham are important in the story of Babel (Gen 10:6-12). Ham had four sons. One of them was Cush, who had a descendant named Nimrod. It's not clear from the genealogy whether Nimrod was Cush's literal son or a great-grandson. Regardless, he was probably a contemporary of Joktan, who was a great-grandson of Shem's son Eber. (If Nimrod was a literal son of Cush, he could have been born later in Cush's long life and still have been a contemporary of Joktan.)

Joktan was a son of Eber, who was a son of Arphaxad, who was a son of Shem (Gen 10:21-25). Genesis 10:30 records that Joktan and his descendants traveled east from Mesha to Sephar.

OVERVIEW

Rather than scattering to fulfill God's commission to take dominion over the earth, some of Noah's descendants gathered in the plains of Shinar. By building a great city and tower, they thought they could make a name for themselves and *not* be scattered throughout the earth. God recognized their potential, and in order to keep them from fulfilling it in a rebellious way, He confused their languages and scattered them anyway, preventing their project from continuing.

SOURCE MATERIAL

- Genesis 11:1-9
- Psalm 2
- Proverbs 21:30

The tower of Babel
Before we get into the story of the tower of Babel, we have to figure out who exactly is being referred to in Genesis 11:2. As the story of the tower of Babel begins, we are told that *somebody*, "they" (Gen 11:2), journeyed from the east. It is often assumed that since Genesis 11:1 says that the whole earth had one language that the "they" of verse 2 means all of the descendants of Noah. This is unlikely for a couple of reasons. First, it says that "they journeyed from the east" (Gen 11:2); if everyone had stuck together after the flood, they would've been coming from the west/north, where the mountains of Ararat are. We already know, however, from a few vers-

Unit 2: Humanity Poisoned

OBJECTIVES

Feel...

- the resonance between the city of Babel and the city of Enoch (Cain's city).
- awe at God's ability to see that His is will done whether people want to cooperate with Him or not.

Understand...

- the origins of languages and people groups from Noah's family.
- the core sin of pride and discontent that was at the root of the Babel rebellion.
- the preservation of the seed-line through Shem's family.

Apply this understanding by...

- considering past situations in your own life where you tried to avoid doing what God wanted, but ended up having to do it anyway.
- considering whether there is a situation in your life now where you are rebelling against God's will.
- considering whether there is a situation in your life where you are seeking your own glory instead of God's.

es before, that Joktan and his descendants had already traveled to the east (Gen 10:30). Those descendants of Shem are the most likely referent of "they" since they were the people group most recently mentioned before the chapter break, and they had already traveled to the east. This is validated by the fact that Abram, a descendant of Joktan's brother, would later come from Ur, which was a short distance from Babel.

But the Joktanites were not alone; Nimrod was a descendant of Cush, and he was ultimately the ruler of the kingdom of Babel (Gen 10:10-11). It seems that Babel may have been built by an alliance between the Joktanites (descendants of Shem) and Nimrod's people (descendants of Ham).

There was nothing wrong with these people coming to the plains of Shinar to live. They demonstrated ingenuity in finding building materials on the plains where there was no stone to quarry and probably not a lot of trees either. Again, no problem at all—they were taking dominion over the earth as God had commanded.

The problem came when, instead of founding scattered settlements across the whole earth the way God had told them, they decided to stay together to build a city, *specifically* so they would not be scattered across the earth. Instead of obeying God, they wanted a city and a tower and—most of all—a reputation. Fulfilling God's mission for them on the earth was not enough for them; they wanted to make a name for themselves (Gen 11:4).

God recognized what they were doing, and His commentary on their achievements and plans in Genesis 11:6 is enlightening. God made humanity creative and capable, and the fall did not take that away. The Bible teaches a very, very high view of human potential, but it also teaches that human potential is not necessarily a good thing.

Of course, God could have let them go on with the project, but then the situation would have escalated just like it had before the fall when God allowed Cain to build a civilization... but this time God had promised not to flood the whole earth. So God mixed up their languages (Gen 11:7), forcing them to do what He had told them to do anyway. Only now they had to obey God out of frustration and impotence rather than freely choosing to be agents of God on the earth. This is an important point of application: sometimes God allows us to disobey, but sometimes He hems us in so that we will ultimately obey Him whether we want to or not. While our choice doesn't hamper God's plans any, it can determine whether we'll be happy and fulfilled in obedience or angry and frustrated in obedience.

Linguistically speaking, it would appear that God confused the languages of the whole world, not just the rebels'. For those who scattered the way they should have, this wouldn't have been a particular problem. Other communities that they didn't interact with now spoke a different language—so what? But for the rebels, it presented such an obstacle that they couldn't continue working together, and construction on the city and tower stopped (Gen 11:8).

We have struggled to try to figure out exactly who the people were who built the tower of Babel, a job that would have been made a lot easier if God had just recorded it in Genesis 11; but there's an important lesson here. The main aim of the tower builders was to make a name for themselves (Gen 11:4), but the Lord in heaven laughs—their story is told, but their names are not recorded (see Psalm 2).

APPLICATION

There is nothing sinful about ambition and accomplishment; the problem with the tower of Babel was twofold. First, they simply didn't want to do what God had told them to—to scatter and populate the earth; this was a simple disobedience problem. The second problem was that they wanted to glorify themselves rather than God.

These two lessons should be applied to any goals and ambitions we might have. Do our ambitions violate any specific direction we have from God (either in His word or regarding our personal calling)? And, do our ambitions aim for God's glory or our own?

ACTIVITIES

1. A Lesson on Language. Think of a time when you have had to interact with someone who didn't speak English (or any language that you know) and answer the following questions.

What was it like to not be able to communicate? Was there some goal you couldn't accomplish because of the language barrier?

Unit 2: Humanity Poisoned

Why do you think God chose to mix up the peoples' languages when they were building the tower of Babel? Was God's strategy effective at stopping them from continuing to build the tower?

2. The Seed-Line Ongoing Activity. Continue the seed-line project you started in Lesson 2.2. Your seed-line paper should have a line of descendants from Adam to Noah, continue vertically down the page from Noah to Abraham following the genealogies in Genesis 10-11. You can add details off to the side if you'd like (brothers of those directly in the seed-line, for example).

Lesson 2.5

EVALUATION

1. What was the sin at the root of the Babel rebellion? _____
_____
_____
_____

2. Was God successful at confusing their languages? _____
_____

3. Did the rebels succeed at disobeying God? _____
_____
_____

4. Did the rebels learn their lesson after God confused their languages? _____
_____
_____

5. How did the Babel rebellion affect the seed-line? _____
_____
_____

www.ingramcontent.com/pod-product-compliance
Lightning Source LLC
Chambersburg PA
CBHW081337080526
44588CB00017B/2657